GRITLOCK

Are the Liberals in Forever?

GRITLOCK

Are the Liberals in Forever?

Peter G. White • Adam Daifallah

Canadian Political Bookshelf,
Toronto

GRITLOCK
Are the Liberals in Forever?

Copyright © 2001, Peter G. White & Adam Daifallah

ISBN: 0-9689374-0-3

Photo of Adam Daifallah by Susan King
Cover photo by Digital Imagery © 2001 Photo Disc, Inc.
Cover design by Karen Petherick, Markham, Ontario

**For more information or
to order additional copies, please contact:**

Canadian Political Bookshelf
10 Toronto St.
TORONTO, Ontario M5C 2B7

tel: (416) 216-0422
fax: (416) 363-4187
web site: *www.gritlock.com*

Printed in Canada by *Essence Publishing*
www.essencegroup.com

Acknowledgments

This book was first contemplated in February 2001, and is on sale eight months later. Since it is aimed at a moving target, we deemed that timeliness and relevance to Canada's contemporary political situation were more important than academic perfection; so the usual disclaimer about any errors being our fault is more than usually appropriate.

As traditional publishers do not operate at that speed, we were fortunate to learn, at the end of June, of a rapidly growing company in Belleville, Ontario — Essence Publishing. We are grateful to David Visser, Gus Henne and their associates at Essence for their willingness to adapt to our timetable. We would also like to thank Karen Petherick of Intuitive Design International Ltd. in Markham, Ontario for her quick and excellent work on the cover design. Distribution was capably handled by Bill Hushion of Hushion House Publishing Ltd., Toronto.

Leading us through the maze of Canada's book business was Bill Hanna, president of Acacia House Publishing Services Ltd. of Toronto, who was initially engaged as our literary agent but quickly became our editorial adviser, business consultant, and friend. Acacia managing director Frances Hanna suggested the title *Gritlock*, and organized and edited the manuscript with judicious care. We are deeply thankful for their help; together they have been our invaluable coaches and guides.

Many helped us with research, either by offering materials or pointing us in the right direction. We would especially like to thank Mark Quinlan, Michael Cooper, Paul Barnes, Hamish Marshall, Derek Leebosh at Environics Research and the staff of Stauffer Library at Queen's University, Kingston, Ontario.

For their encouragement and advice we would like to thank Professors Donald Savoie and Tom Courchene, as well as others in the academic and political worlds who offered advice and constructive comments. We are also very grateful to Nicole Poirier and Anna Garbin for their unfailingly cheerful administrative assistance and technical support.

Toronto historian Michael Bliss (who rejects our assessment that Brian Mulroney's economic record surpassed Pierre Trudeau's) kindly allowed us to quote his view that our description of the blackening of Mulroney's public image "smacks of wounded partisanship".

Finally, Peter White wants to thank especially his wife Mary White – for many things, but above all for allowing their house to be taken over by a parallel National Archives. A dining-room table may yet emerge again from underneath the stacks.

Peter G. White   *Adam Daifallah*
Knowlton, Que   *Kingston, Ont.*

Table of Contents (condensed)

Detailed Table of Contents

*   *   *   *   *

(d) **Toronto Sun** front page headline "MAYOR: I FEAR STOCK
DAY", November 8, 2000

(e) Elinor Caplan claim that Alliance supporters "are Holocaust
deniers, prominent bigots and racists", November 14, 2000

(f) CBC "documentary" by Paul Hunter on Stockwell Day's religious
beliefs, aired on **The National**, November 14, 2000

4) The premature 2000 election - the Liberals seize their opportunity
How to win a modern election campaign: define your opponent's
image, manage the campaign dialogue in your favour, and introduce
wedge issues that divide the enemy forces
The Liberal advantages in the fall of 2000
The 2000 election: a disaster for the Alliance and the Tories;
Ontario gives Jean Chrétien his third majority

*   *   *   *   *

Table of Charts & Graphs

Foreword

This book is intended for three audiences. The first is all the thousands of active members and supporters of both the Canadian Alliance and the Progressive Conservative Party of Canada; they are the people who actually hold the power to heal the major split in Canada's parliamentary opposition which has made our political system so dysfunctional since 1993. The second is the punditocracy — the journalists and commentators who do so much to shape the political opinions of Canadians on a daily basis, in the hope that the doubters and sceptics will see some merit in the case presented here. And the third is the Canadian body politic in general, who need to understand exactly what has gone wrong, and how easily it might be fixed if those responsible truly wanted to fix it.

The core message of the book is a simple, almost desperate plea to the leadership of the two conservative opposition parties to finally "get their act together", as so many Canadians have urged, so that there will be only one serious conservative candidate in each riding in the next election. Those in charge of both these parties bear a heavy responsibility to all Canadians not to stand in the way of the national interest, which is indisputably to rebuild a second national party capable of forming a government, and that can provide a realistic alternative to the Liberal Party of Canada.

There is also an implicit message for francophone Quebecers. For too long, federal elections in Quebec have been polarized into a simplistic battle between "sovereignists" and "federalists". Since 1993, Quebecers have been expected to choose either the Bloc Québécois or the Liberals; there was virtually no middle ground. But many (if not most) Quebecers support neither the professed desire of the Bloc to lead Quebec out of Canada, nor the over-centralized, paternalistic and authoritarian federalism beloved of the Liberal party. In 1997, under an attractive native-son leader in the person of Jean Charest, the Conservatives received 22.2% of the popular vote in Quebec, and actually won five of its 75 seats. Even Albertan Stockwell Day's Canadian Alliance got 6.2% of the Quebec vote in 2000, while fellow Albertan Joe Clark's Progressive Conservatives got 5.6% — a combined total of almost 12%. What many Quebecers want, and what the country needs, is a viable third option — a national party that wants Quebec to remain a part of Canada, but at the same time is deeply respectful of her constitutional rights and her unique challenge as the home of francophone culture and society in North America. With such a party, Quebecers who are not blindly Liberal would have the opportunity to vote for another party which, unlike the Bloc Québécois, might actually form a national government — a government in which Quebec would be properly represented, as it must be in any truly Canadian government.

◇ **CHAPTER ONE**

Are the
Liberals in Forever?

(*Authors' note to the reader:* Chapter 1 is a synopsis of the case
that is developed at greater length in subsequent chapters. It is
intended as a substantial "executive summary" of the rationale
for cooperation between the Canadian Alliance and the federal
Progressive Conservative party, failing which, the authors
contend, the Liberal Party of Canada will never be defeated.)

Does it matter? Should Canadians care that the Liberal Party
now looks virtually certain to hang on to power in Ottawa indefinitely, thanks to the inability of the other four parties either to
break out of their regional or marginal bases, or to cooperate
with one another to create an effective alternative?

Of course we must care, for our current federal political con-
figuration is a recipe for continuing Canada's gradual decline
into administrative complacency and incompetence, economic
mediocrity, and international irrelevance. But before considering
the growing evidence for that bleak prospect, we must first be
very clear on just why, paradoxically, the Liberals have become
virtually unbeatable.

In theory, of course, as Liberal apologists love to remind us, the Liberals *could* lose the next election, just as they could theoretically have lost the last three. But in practice, they didn't, and they likely won't, because of some very hard realities about federal politics that have obdurately shaped every election since 1993 and will continue to do so for the foreseeable future.

CANADA'S FOUR NEW ELECTORAL REALITIES SINCE 1993

The 1993 federal election was a cataclysmic, revolutionary, watershed event. Even today, its full implications are not widely understood and appreciated. It invalidated all the old assumptions about periodic Liberal vulnerability, such as the late Liberal minister Jack Pickersgill's observation that the Tories are like the mumps — you get them once in a lifetime. Indeed, it is conceivable that we will never get them again.

The new electoral realities virtually guarantee uninterrupted Liberal pluralities, if not majorities — a prospect that privately concerns even many committed Liberals themselves

What are these new electoral realities? They are first, the unprecedented regional differentiation of party support since 1993, resulting in only one "national" party, two strong regional parties, and two weak ones, with each of our four traditional regions favouring a different party. Second, and again unprecedented, is the number of ridings where the presence of three strong candidates allows the marginally strongest to win — under our first-past-the-post electoral system — with barely over a third of the popular vote, and sometimes less. (Since 1993, 36 seats have been won with less than 35% of the vote.) Third, as a consequence of the first two factors, comes the unparalleled division of the parliamentary opposition to the Liberals among four stubborn parties, none of which has been able to win more than a pitiful 66 seats since 1988. And fourth, since 1993 we have witnessed an unprecedented ruthlessness on the part of the Liberal Party and their media allies in destroying the media image of their most dangerous opponents, and in abusing all the levers of power in order to cling to office at all costs.

Let's look at these four new realities more closely.

1) Collapse of the Tories and consequent regionalization of party support

In 1993, the foundations of the great Progressive Conservative Party of Canada disintegrated utterly. The party won two seats. The blocs of regional votes that had given Brian Mulroney two historic consecutive majorities deserted the Conservatives, and went to three other parties where they largely remain today. The three regions lost to the Tories are Western Canada, Ontario, and Quebec. In 2000, the West (B.C. to Manitoba, plus the three seats in the Territories) returned 64 Canadian Alliance members in its 91 seats; Ontario elected 100 Liberals out of 103; while of Quebec's 75 seats, 38 went to the Bloc Québécois and 36 to the Liberals. The Tories elected two members in the West, none in Ontario, and one in Quebec. With nine members in the Atlantic provinces, the Tories came fifth and last for the third election in a row, with only 12 seats altogether, their second worst seat showing in history and their lowest popular vote *ever*.

Western Canada: Reform/Canadian Alliance dominant, Liberals a distant second

In Western Canada, in 1988, the Conservatives had taken 40.8% of the popular vote and 48 seats. In 1993, they dropped to 13.4% of the popular vote and zero seats. In 1997 and 2000, their popular vote declined further to 10.5% and 10%, and they won one and two western seats respectively.

Meanwhile, the Reform Party and its successor, the Canadian Alliance, which had won only 7.3% of the vote in the West in 1988 — Reform's first election ever — have improved in each subsequent election. They took 38.2% in 1993, 43% in 1997, and 49.5% in 2000. This was enough to give them 51 western seats in 1993, and to form the Official Opposition in 1997 and 2000, with 60 and 64 western seats respectively. Yet in none of these three elections have they ever won more than two seats *outside* Western Canada, and there is no indication that they could do any better today.

The Liberals have maintained a respectable minority showing in the West, although they are far behind the Alliance and continue to decline. Their western popular vote over the last three elections has been 30%, 27.6% and 25.3%, which gave them respectively 29 of the 89 western and territorial seats in 1993, and 17 of the 91 seats in both 1997 and 2000.

Ontario: Liberals rule, Reform/Canadian Alliance second, having advanced gradually

It is in Ontario, with almost a third of the seats in the House of Commons, that the change has been the most unexpected and dramatic. Prior to 1993, the Tories had always been able to count on an absolute minimum of 17 seats in Ontario, and Ontario had always been at the core of any Conservative government. In 1988, for example, they won 46 Ontario seats; and in both the 1958 and 1984 Tory sweeps, they won 67 Ontario seats.

But in 1993, the Conservatives were completely wiped out there, as in the West, for the first time in Canadian history. Unlike the West, however, the beneficiary of the Tory collapse in Ontario was not Reform, but the Liberal Party. To the astonishment of most pundits, not only did the Liberals take almost every seat in Ontario in 1993, but they repeated the feat in 1997 and 2000. They were helped by the collapse of the NDP after 1988, gaining much of that vote from 1993 on. Over the last four elections, starting with 1988, the Liberal popular vote in Ontario has been 38.9%, 52.9%, 49.5%, and 51.5%. But the presence of three adversaries splitting the non-Liberal vote in the province since 1993 has worked to give the Liberals almost a clean sweep every time — in 2000, 100 of the province's 103 seats.

In 2000, the Canadian Alliance was a distant second in Ontario with 23.6% of the popular vote and two seats. The Tories took 14.4% of the vote, but won no seats. The NDP got 8.3%, and one Ontario seat.

Quebec: Égalité, *but Bloc Québécois in decline, Liberals oozing back, others not a serious factor*

Ever since the death of Macdonald and the advent of Laurier, Quebec had been the Tories' Achilles heel and the Liberals' stronghold. But Brian Mulroney changed that decisively by taking 58 of Quebec's 75 seats in 1984, and 63 in 1988. In 1993, with Mulroney gone and the Conservatives in a rout, the Liberals, with Quebec francophone Jean Chrétien replacing John Turner as their leader, no doubt hoped to regain their traditional hegemony in the province. But Lucien Bouchard's new Bloc Québécois denied them that satisfaction.

What a stroke of fortune for the Liberals, then, that in 1993, against all odds, and despite having a new francophone leader from Quebec, they gained a strong base in Ontario, of all places — more than compensating for Jean Chrétien's surprising failure to recapture Quebec.

The story of Quebec since 1993 is the story of the initial burst of strength and subsequent gradual decline of the Bloc, the post-Charest collapse of the Conservatives — chiefly to the Liberals' benefit — and the slow but steady re-conquest of the province by the Liberals. The popular vote tells the tale. The Bloc has gone from 49.3% to 37.9% to 39.9%; the Tories from 13.5% under Campbell, to 22.2% under Charest, to 5.6% under Clark; and the Liberals from 33% to 36.7% to 44.2%.

A peculiarity of the new party relationships is that the Bloc Québécois, which runs candidates only in Quebec and does not aspire to form the government, still managed to form the Official Opposition in 1993 with its 54 seats — two more than Reform. In 1997, the Bloc fell to 44 seats against 26 for the Liberals in Quebec; in 2000, they took 38 with the Liberals climbing to 36, and the Tories hanging on to one.

Atlantic: three-way split, with Liberals well ahead, Tories second; Alliance weak

As in Quebec, the Liberals have regained strength in the Atlantic region. In 2000, they took 19 of the 32 Atlantic seats, with the NDP taking four and the Conservatives nine. This is up from 11 Liberal seats in 1997.

So today, as in 1993 and 1997, the Liberals still face four small parties in the House, and are still blessed with a weak, divided and regionally compartmentalized opposition. The only region where the Tories are still at all significant is Atlantic Canada, which has only 32 seats, where in 1997 they managed to win 13 seats, but only nine in 2000. As for the NDP, their 13 seats are scattered among B.C., Saskatchewan, Manitoba, Ontario, New Brunswick and Nova Scotia, and everywhere they appear to be in a death spiral.

None of the Liberals' three regionally-based opponents can succeed in breaking out of their home base unless they cooperate with one another — an uncertain prospect at best — thus leaving the Liberals to dominate Ontario unchallenged and to gradually regain Quebec. Indeed, a complete Liberal sweep of both central provinces next time is not out of the question — a clear majority of 178 seats in central Canada alone. With opportunities like that, who needs the West or the Atlantic?

2) Getting into Parliament with less than 35% of the vote

Before 1993, candidates occasionally found themselves in tight three-way races where the winner got barely more than a third of the votes cast. This might occur when equally-matched candidates of the two historic national parties, Liberals and Conservatives, faced a challenge from a locally strong third party. But such three-way races were exceptional, and no third party ever mounted a serious enduring challenge to the only two parties that have ever formed a federal government since 1867.

But again, 1993 changed all that. One of our two national governing parties was destroyed beyond repair, and has yet to be replaced by another national party capable of winning a plurality of seats in Parliament and seats in all regions. As a result, close three-way races have become commonplace, and for the first time we are even seeing a handful of close four-way races.

Some statistics illustrate the difference. In the three federal elections that preceded 1993, only nine candidates won a seat with under 35% of the votes in their riding. In the three elections since 1993, this number has rocketed to 36 — 14 Liberals, 11 NDP, 10 Reform, 1 PC and zero Alliance. This phenomenon has become less pronounced from election to election, as the third and fourth parties in each region by and large continue to weaken: in 1993, there were 18 seats won with less than 35% of the vote; in 1997, there were 14; and in 2000, there were only four. To put it mildly, none of these MPs can claim a strong mandate from their electors.

This is one effect of the notorious "vote-splitting" that Reform and the Canadian Alliance have been complaining about since 1997. While this in itself has not produced the recent Liberal majorities, it has unquestionably contributed to them. For example, if Tory and Alliance votes in 2000 are taken together in every riding and attributed to a single candidate, those candidates would have won 34 seats that in actuality went to the Liberals, and two more that went to the NDP, thereby reducing the Liberal seat total to 138 (a minority in the House), and increasing the combined PC/Alliance total to 114 from its present 78.

The lesson of recent elections is that the presence of two or more strong candidates against a strong Liberal clearly divides the Liberal opposition, and facilitates a Liberal victory with a minority of the vote. This effect has been especially noticeable in Ontario, where the Tories and the Alliance have been battling each other for second place, to the benefit of Liberal candidates. And it is not only "vote-splitting" between these two parties that benefits the Liberals, but also candidate-splitting, money-splitting, worker-splitting and strategist-splitting. In fact, Tory and Alliance strategists have been spending as much time and energy plotting against each other as they have plotting against the Liberals.

But by far the most important effect of the Tory-Alliance rivalry in Ontario has been to provoke the antipathy of many ordinary voters, who simply cannot understand why the two parties do not combine to form a single stronger and more credible alternative to the Liberals. Their reaction is "a plague on both your houses", and they either hold their nose and vote Liberal or else stay home. Most Ontarians do not vote Liberal out of enthusiasm or confidence, but by default. The low repute of the Chrétien government in 2000, compounded by the failure of the opposition parties to present an acceptable alternative, in fact produced the lowest voter turnout in the history of federal elections in Ontario — a mere 58%. The Liberals actually took 100 Ontario seats with the support of only 29.7% of registered Ontario voters. Given that our voter registration system omits many people, the percentage of *eligible* voters would be even smaller — smug critics of low US election turnouts take note.

It is thus misleading to claim, as many do who should know better, that healing the Tory-Alliance split in Ontario would produce only a marginal change. In fact, if done properly, it would reclaim many voters who have been reluctantly voting Liberal, and bring many others back from their living-rooms into the voting booth

3) Weak and divided opposition in the House of Commons

How pleasant to be a Liberal front-bencher since 1993, enjoying the unparalleled spectacle of four pitiable opposition parties, not one of which has the remotest chance of threatening your own party's hold on the government. Today, the 172 members of the Liberal caucus look out on an Official Opposition that is less than 40% their size, with only two members east of Manitoba; a third party (the Bloc) unique to Quebec, that has only 38 members; a fourth party (the NDP) with 13 members, and apparently in its final agony — a demise that could only benefit the Liberal party; and a fifth party (the PCs) with 12 members that is now a ghostly Atlantic shade of its former glory. Better still, the leadership of the four parties shows no signs of taking the bold steps needed to form a stronger opposition, although in the case of the Alliance and the PC parties at least, the vast majority of their supporters would like them to do so. But there are apparently too many egos, too many party jobs and titles, and too many rivalries and grudges among the leadership cliques to allow the interests of the country to come first. Among some

Tories, there is also the misguided belief that they can win back all the Canadian Alliance seats in B.C. and Alberta.

This is the bottom line: until the leadership of both the Progressive Conservatives and the Canadian Alliance either promotes or acquiesces in formal talks about the eventual reunification of their two parties, as a first step to restoring some credibility to the Official Opposition, the Liberals are bound to win election after election. And if the other parties delay this process long enough to allow the Liberals to finish their work of supplanting the Bloc in Quebec while the Alliance and the Tories themselves are too weak and divided to do so, then even their own reunification will be futile. This is a matter of the greatest possible urgency for Canada.

4) The trademark Liberal weapon: ruthless character assassination of opposing leaders

More than any other single factor, the performance of the leader — or more precisely, the public perception of the leader's performance — is the most critical element in the success or failure of a party in a federal election. The dominant role of television, our tendency to imitate US-style campaigns focused on the leader, and the permanent news cycle reporting the various leaders' every move, all reinforce this fact.

Most party leaders enter campaigns with a fairly well defined public image, so that the opportunity to improve or denigrate it during the actual campaign is limited. This is not the case for a newly elected leader who is in the full public spotlight for the first time. Modern campaigns have largely become battles in image definition, where each side tries to define the public perception of the opposing leader in the most negative fashion possible without creating a backlash by going too far, while trying to protect or enhance the perception of its own leader. The team that is most successful in denigrating the opposing leader wins, which is why negative attacks have largely replaced positive campaigns. The public has no inkling of the feverish backstage manoeuvering devoted to shaping its view of each leader leading up to and during a campaign — it sees only the result, with no comprehension of the cynical ways in which its own daily perceptions are being shaped. The media, some of whom are privy to what is really happening behind the scenes, never seem to report on it. Perhaps this is because they themselves are essential participants in the process, whether wittingly or otherwise.

Political image definition is a black art, perfected in the United States, and practised in Canada by a tiny handful of backroom Machiavellis largely hidden from the public eye. For at least the past decade, federal Liberal strategists have been the unchallenged masters of this particular form of character assassination. Although they were always better at it than their adversaries, they began to reach new heights (or depths) dating roughly from the election of Jean Chrétien as Liberal leader in June, 1990. Many members of the national media have enthusiastically joined in, be it because they actually despise their targets, enjoy the power to influence events, or have a political agenda or career interest of their own. The first major victim of the new extremes of image denigration was Prime Minister Brian Mulroney himself, who came to be called "Canada's most hated prime minister" in occasional media references. This vilification of Mulroney culminated in journalist Stevie Cameron's book *On the Take*, subtitled *Crime, Corruption and Greed in the Mulroney Years*, which cites among its sources several Liberal Party operatives still active today.

This was followed by the infamous letter from Canadian Justice Department lawyer Kimberly Prost to Swiss authorities on September 29, 1995, alleging that Mulroney had violated section 121 of the Criminal Code (frauds on the government). The apparent initial basis of her information, and that of the RCMP, was a story by reporter Trish Wood on the CBC television program *The Fifth Estate* in late March 1995, about "secret payments" in connection with Air Canada's purchase of a new fleet from Airbus Industrie. According to William Kaplan's book *Presumed Guilty: Brian Mulroney, the Airbus Affair, and the Government of Canada*, Prost's letter of 11 single-spaced pages identified former Newfoundland premier Frank Moores as an Airbus Industrie lobbyist, and German-Canadian businessman Karlheinz Schreiber as a recipient of commissions from the company, saying, "The RCMP has reliable information that Mr. Schreiber was given these commissions in order to pay Mr. Mulroney and Mr. Moores…" (page 87). Prost then referred to two other allegations of payoffs to Mulroney, concluding, "The above three cases demonstrate an ongoing scheme by Mr. Mulroney, Mr. Moores and Mr. Schreiber to defraud the Canadian government of millions of dollars of public funds from the time Mr. Mulroney took office in September, 1984 until he resigned in June, 1993" (page 89). None of these allegations was true.

No doubt it is possible to argue that Brian Mulroney has suffered no worse at the hands of the image-makers than has Jean Chrétien, and that, in the words of historian and commentator Michael Bliss in a private communication, any contention that non-Liberals such as Mulroney have been singled out "smacks of wounded partisanship." It is unlikely that such a claim could withstand a close examination of the media treatment of each man. Be that as it may, one cannot help comparing the media's near-universal deification of Pierre Trudeau with their widespread demonization of Mulroney, despite the assessment by a number of academic studies that Trudeau's prime ministership was largely an economic disaster, while Mulroney's was one of the most economically successful in Canadian history. Those of us who do not share the conventional view of Trudeau so dear to central Canada's liberal/media establishment can find a precedent in the canonization of John Kennedy by their American counterparts, despite his meagre record. No matter — we accept, as JFK's father once told him, that "life is not fair."

Mulroney's successor as prime minister, the novice Kim Campbell, was personally popular until she called an election in September, 1993. She immediately played into the Liberals' hands by admitting that unemployment would remain high for several years, an honest but naïve statement for which she was promptly crucified. As a neophyte leader, she was easy cannon-fodder for the Liberal image manipulators who successfully defined her as a weak and vain inheritor of the worst aspects of the Mulroney record. She led her party to its worst defeat in history, the defeat from which it has never recovered, and soon left politics.

In 1997, the Liberals' opponents were Preston Manning, Alexa McDonough and Jean Charest, as well as new Opposition Leader Gilles Duceppe in Quebec. Since only Manning had experience in leading his party in a general election, the Liberals concentrated their fire on him, successfully portraying him as a dangerous western radical inimical to the interests of Central and Eastern Canada. Although they could not damage his image in the West, they succeeded brilliantly in making him seem unacceptable to Ontario voters. Charest was more difficult to vilify, but he was never a real threat, and the Liberals contented themselves with drawing him onto the constitutional battleground, a favourite theme of his, which unfortunately was anathema to Ontario after Meech and Charlottetown. Duceppe was made to seem incompetent and ridiculous — first when photographed wearing a hairnet on a factory tour, then because his campaign bus got lost in rural Quebec. Another cakewalk for the Liberals, and one which played no small part in encouraging Jean Charest's early withdrawal to head the Quebec Liberal Party.

This brings us to the election of November 2000, which was the Liberal hatchet-men's finest hour. Their victim this time was the hapless Stockwell Day, elected leader of the Canadian Alliance only weeks earlier, who served both as Jean Chrétien's excuse and his real reason for calling an early election after only three and a half years. It proved to be child's play for the Liberal pros to vilify Day as a fundamentalist western loonie intent on provoking a referendum to outlaw abortion, and on introducing the dreaded "two-tier health care" scheme, among other secret plans on his "hidden agenda" — and he refused to work on Sundays! As Liberal strategist Warren Kinsella explained after the election, the Day team not only allowed Kinsella's group a free hand in defining his image for the Ontario electorate as "scary", but also failed to "manage the dialogue" during the campaign. In other words, Day was knocked off his battle plan four days out of five, and his attacks on Chrétien's integrity were largely ineffective as a result. Once again, Day's party was contained within Western Canada except for a paltry two seats in Ontario, while the Liberals increased their majority once more.

The lesson of the last ten years is that the Liberal party has become absolutely ruthless in moving to destroy the public image and credibility of anyone whom they perceive as a possible threat — often before the targets know what hit them. Liberal spinners play the media like a violin, planting innuendoes and manufacturing suspicions. Since 1993, with their huge built-in advantage as masters of the entire apparatus of government, they can be smoothly and invisibly effective in eliminating or co-opting potential sources of danger, or in propping up weak opponents to prevent stronger ones from emerging. Any Canadian who aspires to knock the Liberals from their perch must be well prepared for these attacks, and be skilful and resolute in deflecting them.

A LIBERAL CANADA IN THE TWENTY-FIRST CENTURY: DRIFT, DECLINE AND DECAY

What is happening to our country? Where have these invulnerable Liberals brought us since 1993, and where will they take us in the future?

The answer is that while the Liberals soothingly assure us that the country is in great shape, that everything is for the best in this best of all possible worlds, in reality Canada is gradually, almost imperceptibly, sliding into mediocrity and irrelevance. Concerned only with ruthlessly maintaining itself in power, the Liberal Party is offering no national focus and direction, no challenging goals or inspiring expectations, not even sound management of the economy — in short, it is failing to provide vital national leadership. Meanwhile, the signs of hidden rot and decay are growing ever more visible and widespread.

While for years the Liberals have boasted of Canada's ranking first (now third) in the UN Human Development Index, and of our lowest cost of living among the G7 nations, they prefer to ignore a host of inconvenient but sobering realities, of which we will highlight only three.

1) Canada's declining relative standard of living

There are two accepted measures of living standards: average personal income per capita (before taxes), and real disposable income per capita (after taxes). By both measures, Canada is continuing to fall farther and farther behind the United States, and other countries as well.

In 2000, Canada's personal income per capita was only 78.3% of that in the United States, down from 87.2% a decade earlier. In terms of disposable income, Canadians were at only 70.3% of the American level in 2000, down from 79.3% in 1989, because of our higher tax burden. According to former Royal Bank economist (and now Liberal MP) John McCallum, during the decade of the 1990s our living standards, as measured by real disposable income per capita, actually *fell* by 2%, while American living standards rose by 18%. McCallum concluded that if these trends were to continue, Canada's standard of living will have fallen to a mere 50% of US levels by 2010. He pointed out (before becoming a Liberal candidate) that with the pre-vailing status quo/business-as-usual attitude in Ottawa, there is a real prospect of continued relative income deterioration. His presence on the government benches today is an instructive example of the Liberals' skill in co-opting their critics.

2) Canada's declining relative productivity

Although during the 1990s both Canada and the US experienced growth in labour productivity (as measured by gross domestic product per worker), from 1989 to 2000 Canada's productivity rose by an average of only 1.2% a year, well below the 1.9% average in the US. As a result, output per worker in Canada has fallen from 85% of that in the US in 1989 to only 79% in 2000. Most of the increase in this gap occurred in the second half of the decade, under the Liberal government, despite some improvement following the recession of the early 1990s. The problem is that the Canadian improvement in the second half came nowhere near to matching the huge productivity growth in the US, at 2.83% a year from 1996. This US surge in productivity is generally credited to new information technology, of which the US has been both the major producer and the leading user.

The productivity gap also reflects an innovation gap with the US, as evident from Canada's relatively much lower research and development spending and the relatively fewer patents obtained by Canadians during the period in question

Fifteen years ago, Canada's GDP per capita (another measure of productivity) was two and a half times that of Ireland. Today, Ireland's per capita GDP is 10% to 15% higher than ours. Whereas in 1990 Canada ranked third in the world in GDP per capita, by 1998 we fell to fifth in the world, overtaken by Denmark and Norway.

3) Canada's declining dollar relative to the US

Partly as a consequence of our growing productivity gap with the US, the Canadian dollar has declined from 87 cents US in 1991 to around 65 cents today. Our dollar has lost more than a third of its value relative to the US in only 30 years, and has become an international liability for Canadian travellers and investors. While Prime Minister Chrétien may say that our low dollar helps Canadian exporters, what he does not say is that it reduces the international value of our capital assets (thereby encouraging foreign takeovers), makes it harder for Canadian firms to attract and retain the best workers, and reduces purchasing power for all Canadians. According to Michael Porter of the Harvard Business School and Dean Roger Martin of Toronto's Rotman School of Management, the decline in the value of our currency is equivalent to a cut in pay of over 20% for every Canadian.

CONCLUSION

We have not mentioned Canada's health care imbroglio, our high taxes, the disengagement of many of our citizens from the political process, or the dangers inherent in restricting the management of our national affairs only to the small number of Canadians who are prepared to join the Liberal Party of Canada. Nor have we considered the inertia and paralysis that inevitably overtake a tired and worn-out party that has been too long in office without a period of renewal; or the lack of incentive or motivation to strive for excellence, and the resulting acceptance of incompetence and personal agendas, both in cabinet and the public service; or the lack of political accountability that leads to favouritism, patronage, corruption and misappropriation of tax dollars. The inevitable product of this situation is the "Who's to stop us?" attitude of many current Liberal ministers, echoing their predecessor C.D. Howe's notorious indiscretion of 1951.

Finally, Canada's increasing insignificance in world affairs and world trade beyond North America would make Lester Pearson ashamed of the party he once led. Instead of aspiring to a strong and independent global role for Canada, the Liberal government seems to be interested mainly in ever-closer integration with the United States.

If the Canadian Alliance and the Progressive Conservatives do not come together in some fashion before the next election, preferably joined by those supporters of the Bloc Québécois who are not hardcore separatists, the Liberal Party will continue to preside indefinitely over Canada's ongoing descent into mediocrity. Whoever would stand in the way of this essential rapprochement will have much to answer for, and must be held accountable for their obstruction.

◇ **CHAPTER TWO**

What is Wrong with Perpetual Liberal Rule?

There may be some Canadians who accept with equanimity the prospect of unchallenged Liberal governments ad infinitum. The authors are happy to report that they don't know any. In fact, it is reassuring that they even know many Liberals who have grave concerns about today's weak, divided and regionalized opposition in Canada, although naturally they do not see it as their job to correct the situation.

Why should Canadians be concerned about perpetual government by one party? There are at least five inter-related reasons: the tendency of any unchallenged authority to abuse its power; to develop a culture of mediocrity leading to decline; to sink into a paralysis or bankruptcy of policy; to rule by clique; as a consequence, to discourage citizen engagement in the political process.

The best short explanation was given in 1887 by British statesman Lord Acton: power tends to corrupt. He added that absolute power corrupts absolutely; but Canada is not quite at this terminal stage. British prime minister William Pitt the elder made the same observation a century earlier: unlimited power is apt to corrupt the minds of those who possess it. This corruption of the mind has been well described as the arrogance of power, and Liberal ministers are not immune from this near-universal human failing. As mentioned at the end of Chapter 1, Louis St. Laurent's minister of trade and commerce, C.D. Howe, once actually taunted the opposition about their powerlessness to stop the Liberal government from doing whatever it wanted.

ABUSE OF OFFICE

The chief danger, and frequently the reality, of such omnipotence is abuse of office. Wherever politicians and their bureaucrats have a monopoly or have exclusive rights, wherever they have arbitrary authority coupled with the conviction that no one can stop them, there is bound to be abuse of this unrestricted power, in matters high and low. The courts, which are the theoretical bulwark against such abuses, are of little help to any but the most rich and powerful among us, in any situation where the government is willing to further abuse our taxes by spending unlimited money and time to defend its initial abuse relentlessly — an advantage that no private citizen can overcome. Even such titans as Conrad Black and Brian Mulroney have personally felt the vengeful sting of the Chrétien government as it deals with its perceived enemies. But it is the myriad of less visible abuses of government authority that happen every day in Canada, and against which the victims have no effective recourse whatsoever, that must concern every Canadian who believes in freedom, due process, and the rule of law.

When the authority of an office is abused so as to benefit the office-holder directly or indirectly, the abuse becomes outright corruption. Political scientist Donald Savoie, in his book *Governing from the Centre: The Concentration of Power in*

Canadian Politics, has demonstrated that the Canadian prime minister is the most powerful elected figure in any democracy, as he enjoys complete authority over both the executive and the legislative branches of the government, and personally appoints and dismisses both cabinet ministers and senior public servants. Jean Chrétien clearly abused his office in personally pressuring the head of the Business Development Bank of Canada to approve a loan to businesses with which he had been associated, in contravention of the Bank's guidelines and recommendations. He and other ministers routinely divert huge sums of taxpayers' money for their own partisan political advantage, even though they may not personally gain a direct financial benefit. They prefer to follow the advice of the Tammany Hall political boss in New York who once said that with all the grand opportunities around for someone with political pull, only a fool would actually steal.

An example of the Liberals' abuse of office and public funds for partisan advantage was the $700 million "Atlantic Investment Partnership" announced less than four months before writs were issued for the 2000 election. According to the website of the Atlantic Canada Opportunities Agency (ACOA), this new program was unveiled at a news conference in Halifax on June 29, 2000, by Prime Minister Chrétien, along with the four (!) regional ministers for Atlantic Canada. The website says this program is "a five-year, $700 million initiative designed to build new partnerships that will increase the capacity of Atlantic Canadians to compete in an increasingly global, knowledge-based economy. Through the Atlantic Investment Partnership, the Government of Canada will make major investments in the areas of innovation, community economic development, trade and investment, and entrepreneurship and business skills development." That should pretty well have covered the Atlantic waterfront.

The $700 million that Canadian taxpayers contributed to the Atlantic Investment Partnership worked out to $603 for every voter in the region. But it was only the tip of the iceberg of Liberal largesse to the Atlantic region. Net transfers to the Atlantic provinces from the rest of Canada (via Ottawa) equal about 30% of their GDP; yet unemployment levels there are still the highest in the country. Indeed, many economists argue that the Employment Insurance program, as presently structured, encourages unemployment and underemployment instead of decreasing it, and that compared to the rest of Canada, the Atlantic region is actually worse off than it was 30 years ago. The main effect of these massive transfers (not necessarily an unintended one) has been to build up a culture of dependence on discretionary and politically determined grants from Ottawa, creating a tacit understanding that ridings and provinces that vote Liberal in federal elections will continue to receive immense federal payments.

An even more blatant example of the Liberals' abuse of office for electoral advantage was the announcement on September 20, 2000 — a month before the election call — by Human Resources Development Minister Jane Stewart, of the reversal of the Liberal government's own much-needed 1996 reforms in the costly, overly-generous and incentive-destroying Employment Insurance program. By once again making EI cheques easy to qualify for, the Liberals' attempt to buy votes in the Atlantic provinces with public funds was apparently successful.

A related example of abuse of office and public funds for partisan gain is the entire jobs grants program at Human Resources Development Canada, where up to $1 billion in grants were mismanaged. The Auditor General reported that the performance of HRDC was "disturbing", involving "breaches of authority, improper payments, limited monitoring and approvals that had not followed established procedures." This is bureaucratese for saying that many grant recipients were selected on the basis of politically motivated recommendations from Liberal MPs and party officials.

Public office may also be abused for the purpose of persecuting one's political enemies. The most notorious example of the use of this tactic by the Chrétien government was the politically motivated RCMP investigation into unsubstantiated rumours of kickbacks to former prime minister Brian Mulroney in relation to the purchase by Air Canada of 34 Airbus A320 jets from Airbus Industrie. It took a major libel action and a professional public relations campaign by Mulroney, at a personal cost of over $2 million, to clear his name. Although the Liberal government was forced to allow the RCMP to pay Mulroney's expenses, it still has not halted the RCMP investigation.

Finally, it is also abuse of office, and a major waste of taxpayers' money, to proceed with reckless political undertakings made in opposition, no matter how misguided they may turn out to be in government. Two egregious examples of such politically motivated and expensive decisions by the Chrétien Liberals illustrate this point. The first was the cancellation in 1993 of the previous government's contract to buy new EH-101 helicopters to replace some 30 Sea King ship-borne helicopters, then 37 years old. The second was the similar cancellation of a contract with a private-sector company — Don Matthews' Paxport Inc., which later joined its rival, Charles Bronfman's Terminal 3 group, to form the Pearson Development Corporation — to manage passenger terminals at Pearson International Airport in Toronto. The first breach of contract has cost Canadian taxpayers at least $600 million, and the second, far more.

MEDIOCRITY AND DECLINE

A second danger of unbroken one-party government is mediocrity, leading to decline in comparison to countries where true political competition produces better government. In the absence of any serious competition, the Liberals have no incentive to excellence or to innovation. There is no sense of urgency, and little imagination. Drift and decline set in, as the perquisites of power exercise their seduction, as ministers and MPs devote their attentions and energies to the ceaseless jockeying to replace their leader or to ensure their positions under his successor, and as boredom, inattention and laziness take their toll on a team too long in place. The few talented MPs among the hordes of time-serving government backbenchers become increasingly frustrated, since the prime minister has no incentive to renew and reinvigorate his cabinet, and indulgently tolerates such mediocrities as Elinor Caplan (see **BACKGROUNDER 3C** below), or such national embarrassments as Hedy Fry (who has never explained her bizarre claim that crosses were burning on lawns in Prince George, British Columbia).

Three devastating examples of Canada's decline under the current Liberal government are the drop in our relative purchasing power, standard of living and overall competitiveness vis-à-vis the United States; the deterioration of our health care system; and the downgrading of our armed forces.

1) Canada is falling farther behind the US

According to economist Tom Courchene in his recent book, *A State of Minds: Toward a Human Capital Future for Canadians*, "real purchasing power of adult Canadians, relative to adult Americans, reached a peak of near 84 per cent in the late 1970s. By 1998, purchasing power had tumbled to a low of almost 70 per cent" (page 208). Courchene cites a 2000 Industry Canada study which says that one third of US states have a standard of living more than 25 per cent higher than the Canadian average, while five Canadian provinces (Manitoba and the Atlantic provinces) rank below Mississippi, the state with the lowest standard of living. The wealthiest states, such as Delaware or Connecticut, have living standards 50 per cent above the Canadian average.

Other worrisome economic failings noted by Courchene:

* Canada's share of foreign direct investment in North America has fallen from roughly 27 per cent in 1985 to only 15 per cent in 1998 (page 213).

* Despite the Liberal plan to reduce corporate tax rates from 28 to 21 per cent over five years, our rates are still much higher than the United States' and are not competitive (page 223).

* Our extremely low dollar ensures Americans bargain-basement prices for Canadian assets, contributing to the ongoing buyout of corporate Canada and the shortfall in relative productivity (page 249).

* Many of our brightest and most talented young Canadians are migrating (page 228).

Courchene concludes that we "run the serious risk of becoming an 'incubator' economy for the US and other foreign multinationals and, in the process, we will erode our ability to grow big business within Canada" (page 223).

2) Our health care system is in disarray

The state of Canada's shattered and bureaucratically strangled health care system is too well known to require description. But it is nonetheless sobering to compare our situation with other countries. While the OECD ranked Canada fifth among its 29 member countries in national health expenditure, we fell into the bottom third of countries for availability of medical technology such as MRI and CT scanners. This is an indication of the inefficient distribution of resources that is inevitable in a monolithic command and control structure, where only the most restricted role is permitted for the private sector, where normal healthy competition is prevented from improving efficiency, and where powerful public sector unions, not accountable to doctors or patients, exert far too much influence. The Harvard School of Public Health found that 67 per cent of Canadian specialists think the quality of care has declined — the highest percentage in the five countries it surveyed.

Although the original intent of the Canada Health Act was that costs would be shared 50/50 between Ottawa and the provinces, Ottawa's cash share is now only 14 per cent of total public health spending in the country, down from 18 per cent before the Paul Martin cuts of up to $6.2 billion in annual federal transfers which began in 1994-95. That represents a 22 per cent drop in the federal commitment. For the federal government to reach an 18 per cent share again, it would need to contribute an additional $8 billion annually by 2004-05. As a result of federal cutbacks, the typical province now spends roughly 30% of its total budget on health care — the largest single budget item, just ahead of debt service.

In dollar terms, the federal government provided the provinces with $18.7 billion in Canadian Health and Social Transfers (CHST) in the year before the Martin cuts began. By 1999, it had cut annual CHST cash entitlements by $6.2 billion, or 33%. It restored only $2 billion of these cuts in 1999-2000, leaving an ongoing shortfall of $4.2 billion as compared to five years earlier, without even taking cost increases into account.

3) Our military is in decline

Both the Canadian Alliance and the Progressive Conservative party agree that the condition of Canada's military is bordering on desperate, and is now a national disgrace, considering its great history and traditions. The following assessment is from a recent Canadian Alliance policy paper:

> The Canadian Armed Forces are today in a state of crisis. While our troops are being asked to serve in increasingly numerous and dangerous conflict zones overseas — such as Kosovo, Bosnia and East Timor — they remain inadequately equipped. Deep and systemic problems in the capabilities of the Canadian Armed Forces are not being addressed. The Conference of Defence Associations, the Auditor General and other independent analysts have catalogued some of the most serious problems:
>
> * Capital equipment requirements face a shortfall of up to $30 billion by 2012.
>
> * For years, there was a deficit of some $1.5 billion in resources available for training and related functions.
>
> * Manpower in the regular forces has fallen by about 25 per cent over the past seven years and numbers continue to drop.
>
> * The Army has been described as in a "state of near collapse" with soldiers in some units serving continuous rotations overseas with virtually no rest at home.
>
> * The Militia is in an especially bad condition and requires additional funding simply to pay people, to acquire equipment, and to train properly.

* Personnel continue to leave the forces in large numbers due to policies that compromise operational effectiveness, and a perception that government does not take their role seriously.

* In 2000-01, only $55 million in new funding is being provided for capital equipment. According to the Conference of Defence Associations, the additional money is less than 50 per cent of what would be needed to address the broader basis of the crisis in the Canadian Forces.

POLICY PARALYSIS

A third danger is paralysis of policy. In the absence of new people with new ideas, policy generation becomes unimaginative and stagnant. What few good new ideas might be advanced are generally ignored, while bad new ideas (such as the prime minister's pet project of "Millennium Scholarships") are seldom questioned, challenged or changed. With no reason to be proactive, the government's watchword becomes "steady as she goes". Policy is guided by polling data, and by electoral considerations, as the Liberals are not shy to pilfer the best proposals of other parties. In today's highly competitive global community, where there can be no refuge from worldwide trends and pressures, such complacent, self-absorbed and negligent leadership has become disastrous for Canada. As mentioned in the previous chapter, while the prime minister was boasting about Canada's UN rating as "the best country in the world" (now third best), he ignored our declining standard of living, our declining productivity and our declining dollar as compared with those of the United States.

A frustratingly typical example of the paralysis of policy development is the federal government's refusal to consider a wider role for the private sector in providing health care services to Canadians. This makes Canada one of the few countries in the developed world where private health care is all but illegal. It is indisputable that the private sector can provide many health care services more efficiently and cheaply than the sclerotic and union-dominated monopoly public sector, thus reducing waiting periods and costs. But the Liberal government's blind adherence to its own narrow interpretation of the Canada Health Act, against the wishes of many provinces who are the legal providers of health care, forces many desperate Canadians to seek private care outside the country. This is not the leadership the country needs — it is electorally-motivated followership at its worst.

A corollary to the lack of new policy initiatives is the tendency to perpetuate old, discredited and simply bad policies. We have mentioned massive wealth transfers to Atlantic Canada, and aspects of the Employment Insurance program which encourage dependency and discourage initiative. We might also include policies concerning aboriginal peoples or First Nations, which have failed abysmally to address most of the real problems and challenges facing these Canadian citizens, and have instead frequently exacerbated them.

GOVERNMENT BY CLIQUE

A fourth danger of permanent Liberal rule is government by clique, and exclusion of all who are not members of the clique. The long Liberal hegemony has created a small, self-perpetuating oligarchy or aristocracy of governors, from which the vast majority of Canadians are permanently excluded, and to which only bona fide members of the Liberal party may expect to accede. Since power in the Liberal party is concentrated in Ontario and Quebec (the source of all its leaders), or even more narrowly in Toronto and Montreal, few outsiders need apply. The Liberal near-monopoly of power in Ottawa has also had the effect of moulding most of the public service in the party's image, since the hiring and promotion of most of our public servants takes place under Liberal regimes. Another effect has been the defection to other arenas, such as provincial politics or the private sector, of many outstanding and public-spirited Canadians who are denied the opportunity to participate in the governance of their country simply because they are not Liberals, or could not bring themselves to become so. This has meant a vast loss of potential talent that in most nations would be welcomed and highly motivated to serve in the government of their country. One of the reasons for the comparative vigour of the US government is the constitutional limit of two four-year terms for each president. This rule brings a wholesale change in the administration at least every eight years, attracting dynamic and motivated men and women who know they have a limited time to make their mark, fight for their causes, and advance their dreams.

Professor Savoie's book *Governing from the Centre*, mentioned earlier, gives a timely analysis of the unprecedented concentration of power in the hands of the current prime minister. He says (page 79) that government candidates in elections "have little choice but to adopt the policies of the prime minister as prepared by a handful of his most trusted advisers rather than the policies of the party, to which all members were able to contribute." He points out that Jean Chrétien has abolished a large number of cabinet committees, including Priorities and Planning, and cabinet meetings have become a time where "briefings are presented, information is shared, and where the prime minister and certain ministers provide a general *tour d'horizon*" (page 127). As one Chrétien cabinet minister called it, the cabinet is now a "kind of focus group for the prime minister" (page 260). The Prime Minister's Office now exerts exorbitant amounts of control over the entire parliamentary process, and "Cabinet has now joined Parliament as an institution being bypassed. Real political debate and decision making are increasingly elsewhere..." (page 362).

CITIZEN DISENGAGEMENT

A fifth danger, which became more evident in the last election, is the withdrawal from the political process of more and more Canadians, and especially young people. In an electoral system that offers no real hope of a change in government, many Canadians see no point in voting at all. As we saw in Chapter 1, the turnout in Ontario in the 2000 federal election, when none of the four parties was particularly attractive to the voters, was a miserable 58% of registered voters — an all-time record low.

Continuing uninterrupted and unchallenged Liberal rule is a recipe for the continuing gradual drift, decline and decay of our country. Only the presence of a strong and united opposition in the House and in every region — an opposition that is truly respected and feared by the Liberals instead of routinely disdained and ignored — can force the government to be truly accountable to Canadians, and either deliver or be replaced.

THE UNACCEPTABLE DISCREPANCY BETWEEN CANADA'S PERFORMANCE AND ITS POTENTIAL, AS SEEN BY THE CONFERENCE BOARD OF CANADA

Perhaps the most reputable and impartial organization to have analyzed Canada's socio-economic performance continuously over recent years is the Conference Board of Canada. The Conference Board does not lobby governments, nor does it make policy prescriptions. But every year since 1996, the Conference Board has published a report comparing Canada's performance with that of other countries, showing where we are succeeding, and where we are failing to do as well as our competitors.

The report for 2000-01, published in October 2000 shortly before the election, confirms the warnings mentioned above: "As we enter the 21st century, we are at the top of our game. The economy is performing very well, unemployment is nearing record lows, incomes are rising and our governments have been successful in getting their financial affairs on a sustainable footing. But while we are doing well, our comparator countries are doing better. Thus, we remain challenged in a fundamental way: when we are doing so well, it is difficult to mobilize public opinion to accept changes that are needed in order to retain what we have and to build upon it. (…) We continue to point out that our industrial performance needs improvement — manufacturing productivity growth has been well below that of the United States, especially in the last half of the 1990s. Our international competitiveness is far too dependent on a low dollar. Our national innovation record continues to lag [behind] that of other countries, while our record on environmental indicators — a new part of this year's report — shows us turning in a poor performance there as well. Our income per capita, perhaps the most important indicator of how we are doing, is growing; however it is growing *less quickly* than that of our southern neighbour. We believe that the size of the gap is getting to the point where it is more difficult to argue that it is offset by other elements we value as a society."

The Conference Board uses 40 different indicators grouped in six categories, as compared to only three indicators used by the United Nations in Mr. Chrétien's beloved Human Development Index. The report says that among the seven comparable countries studied (Canada, United States, Japan, Germany, Australia, Sweden and Norway), Canada is a top performer in only one category — labour markets — and a relatively poor performer on innovation and the environment. We are average in the economy, in education and skills, and in health and society.

In considering Canada's performance over time, the Conference Board report says, "Taking the 'long view' can be sobering. In 1976, Canadians enjoyed an income per capita, in purchasing power parity terms, that placed us number 3 in an OECD ranking of 26 countries; the United States was number 1. By 1998, this ranking had slipped to seventh out of 29 countries; the United States was number 2. The same comparison using market exchange rates to adjust Canadian income per capita shows that our ranking fell from number 4 in 1976 — just ahead of the United States as number 5 — to number 19 in 1998, with the United States at number 2."

After emphasizing that the real point of its benchmarking exercise is to assess whether Canada is living up to its potential, the Conference Board concludes, "...in comparison to our peers, we can and should do much better."

Why the Alliance and the PCs Must Cooperate

Common Interests, Need for a Single Alternative
in Every Riding, Electoral Fit

Canada can have no strong and united opposition to the Liberals until the Canadian Alliance and the Progressive Conservative party find some way to come together again as one. In addition to their duty to consider the national interest, the two parties have largely common policies and political interests, and many reasons to combine their efforts. Although the combined total of 78 seats won by both parties in 2000 is still small, these 78 seats do in fact include MPs from every province except Prince Edward Island. A caucus formed of the Alliance and Conservative MPs combined could immediately and justifiably claim to be a truly national party, no longer open to dismissal as a mere regional bloc. This fact alone would increase the party's appeal for many voters, especially in Ontario, who are reluctant to support a party identified with only one region of the country.

The Canadian Alliance and the Progressive Conservatives are both democratic conservative parties. They are both parties of the centre or centre-right, despite attempts to portray the Alliance as a right-wing party, or the Tories as a left-wing party. It is sometimes alleged that the fundamental principles or policies of the two parties are so different that they could never work together. This view cannot be supported on the evidence of the two official party programs, which are the only formal enunciations of party policy. The following point-by-point comparison of the electoral program of each party for the 2000 election demonstrates the high degree to which their policies are similar or at least not incompatible. The Canadian Alliance platform was entitled *A Time for Change: An Agenda of Respect for All Canadians*. The Progressive Conservative platform was called *Change You Can Trust: The Progressive Conservative Plan for Canada's Future.*

Comparison of the 2000 election programs of the Progressive Conservative Party and the Canadian Alliance

PC PARTY	CANADIAN ALLIANCE
— TAXATION —	
• Raise the Basic Personal Exemption to $12,000 by the year 2005.	• Raise the Basic Exemption to $10,000.
• Raise the married and equivalent-to-spouse exemption on income tax to $12,000 (single-income families, including single parents, will not have to pay tax on their first $24,000 of income).	• A single rate of 17% for income up to $100,000 and a rate of 25% for anything above, as well as scrapping the 5% income surtax. A family of four would not pay tax on the first $26,000 of income.
• A $1,176 per year child tax deduction (equal to a $200 tax cut).	• A $3,000 per year universal child tax deduction.
• Completely repeal personal capital gains tax.	• Raise the Spousal Exemption to $10,000.
• Lower the capital gains inclusion rate for business to 50%.	• Cut the capital gains inclusion rate to 50%.
• Ensure there is tax neutrality for non-resident investment in Canadian e-businesses.	• Cut technology and service industry taxes from 28% to 21%.
• Cut corporate rates to the OECD average – about 20.5%.	• Cut small business tax rate from 12% to 10% on the first $200,000 of income.

PC PARTY	CANADIAN ALLIANCE
— TAXATION —	
• Cut the federal excise tax on diesel fuel by half for a one-year period.	• Cut the federal excise tax on farm diesel fuel by half.
• Reduce the federal excise tax by four cents per litre on low sulphur fuels for a two-year period.	• Eliminate the "temporary" 1.5 cent/litre increase in federal excise tax on gasoline.
• Remove the GST on home heating fuels for a period of one year.	• Cut the GST on top of other federal and provincial fuel taxes.
• Double to $800 the value of the tax credit currently given to Canadians who care for a low-income elderly parent, grandparent, or infirm relative in their home.	• Decrease EI rates for employees from $2.40 to $2.00 per $100 earned, and for employers, from $3.36 to $2.80 per $100 earned.
• Make the disability tax credit refundable, extending the disability tax credit to persons with disabilities but without taxable income.	
— REGULATORY REFORM —	
• "Work toward the cooperative elimination of excessive regulation, overlap, duplication and waste in the allocation of responsibilities between the federal and provincial/territorial governments."	
• Implement an annual "Red Tape Budget" which would detail the estimated total cost of each individual regulation.	
• "Work toward ensuring that user fees that are tied to regulatory approval are limited to no more than the cost of actually providing that approval."	
• "Require each department wishing to enact a new regulation to first have conducted an independent review of the economic impact and compliance costs."	

PC PARTY	CANADIAN ALLIANCE
— REGULATORY REFORM —	
• "Ensure that all proposed regulations are put on the departmental web site for thirty days to allow for greater public awareness before they are published in the *Canada Gazette*." • "Work with provincial governments to development a uniform approach to securities regulations."	
— NATIONAL DEBT —	
• Legislate repayment. • Pay off $25 billion in the first five years with the goal of having debt completely eliminated in 25 years.	• Legislate repayment. • Pay down at $6 billion per year, with increases "as we can afford it".
— RRSPs —	
• Increase foreign content limit from 25% to 50%.	• Increase the foreign content limit (no specific amount offered). • Increase the contribution limit to 30% of income, up from the current 18%.
— HEALTH CARE —	
• "Immediately restore the ash portion of the Canada Health and Social Transfer to at least 1993-94 levels. • Establish a sixth principle of the Cananda Health Act for 'stable fubding'. • "Work with the provinces in creating targets and goals for the system and to develop a Wellness Agenda stressing health promotion and disease prevention. • "Work with the provinces to develop national standards for a Canada-wide health info-system to bring a greater level of accessibiltiy and accountability to the health care system."	• Give full restoration of health transfers to the 1995 level of $18.7 billion, and stable, guaranteed funding in the future. • Maintain the five principles of the Canada Health Act; adopt a more cooperative approach in working with the provinces. • Guarantee in law long-term funding through five-year funding agreements with a "funding escalator," ensuring that unilateral federal cuts cannot happen again. • Work with provinces to develop national standards of care.

PC PARTY	CANADIAN ALLIANCE
— HEALTH CARE —	
• "Work with the provinces and licensing colleges to seek solutions to the credential problems of foreign-trained doctors."	• Negotiate improved information gathering and reporting between provinces so that citizens from coast to coast can see how their health care measures up.
• "Assist provinces in recruiting medical personnel, particularly for the more sparsely populated areas of the country."	• Keep choice in and freedom to use natural health care products.
• "Work with the provinces to build and develop the most viable models to deliver health care using new technologies, and develop a Canadian strategy for funding and the integration of telehealth into health care delivery."	
• Emphasis on providing better health care for rural Canadians.	
• Work toward a law requiring the labelling of all genetically modified foodstuffs and products for human consumption.	
• Provide a $500 per year tax credit to all Emergency Service Volunteers.	
— JUSTICE —	
• Eliminate conditional sentences for those who commit violent or sexual crimes.	• "Eliminate conditional sentences for violent offenders."
• Bring in more effective youth justice legislation based on protection of the public, deterrence and denunciation balanced with rehabilitation, and a greater discretionary use of restorative justice.	• "Require lifetime supervision for repeat sexual or violent offenders."
	• "Automatic dangerous offender status for a third violent or sexual offence."
• Adopt the principle of discretionary consecutive sentencing for multiple murders.	• Ensure "consecutive rather than concurrent sentences for multiple violent offences."
	• Automatically send 16 and 17 year olds to adult court, as well as 14 and 15 year olds charged with the most serious crimes.

PC PARTY	CANADIAN ALLIANCE
— JUSTICE —	
• "Priority is to defeat organized crime, in particular money laundering, human and contraband smuggling, fraud and computer crime."	• Zero tolerance policy for drugs in federal prisons.
• Improve working conditions and ensure stable funding for the RCMP.	• Make transfer to minimum-security institutions contingent on "good behaviour and completion of rehabilitation programs."
• "Move to cost-sharing with the provinces the youth justice programs on a 50/50 basis, to be phased in over five years."	• Take whatever action is necessary to uphold Canada's current law against child pornography in the face of those who would allow greater access to child pornography in the name of free speech.
• "Establish clear guidelines for communications between schools and the justice system involving young offenders and ensure parents are involved in court proceedings."	• Repeal Bill C-68 concerning the registration of firearms.
• Create a national sex offender registry.	• Increasing funding for rehabilitation and education of drug addicts.
• Create a national strategy to combat child pornography, child abuse and elder abuse.	• Create a national sex offender registry.
• Repeal long gun registration.	• Implement a National Drug Strategy to give police the tools they need to investigate organized crime, and "seize and sell the assets of gangs and other convicted drug dealers."
• "Expand the taking of DNA at the time of arrest to optimize the identification of criminals in unsolved crimes."	• Take steps to curtail illegal immigration and "people smuggling".
• Create a National Victims' Ombudsman Office to ensure victims "have a voice in the federal corrections system", and give victims greater say in the parole process.	
• Replace statutory release with mandatory review reversing the onus to the offender to satisfy the National Parole Board of readiness for release.	
• "Increase the sentence range for crimes involving weapons."	

PC PARTY	CANADIAN ALLIANCE
— JUSTICE —	
• "Create a separate offence for home invasion, swarming and recruitment of children for a criminal purpose." • Streamline the system to make it more user friendly and quick.	
— EMPLOYMENT INSURANCE —	
• Work toward a proposal that would move towards the establishment of individual EI Accounts and an EI Rebate program which would enable workers to roll a portion of their EI contributions into an RRSP upon retirement. • "Support the continuation of an independent Employment Insurance Commission and its role in recommending sustainable EI premiums." • "Review eligibility criteria for skills training and upgrading with the provinces so that all of those who are in need are able to qualify for help."	• Reduce EI rates for employers and employees. • "Encourage shorter and less frequent reliance on EI." • "Workers and employers who draw on the system less will pay lower premiums." • "Workers in similar circumstances will be treated the same way, regardless of where they live in Canada."
— REGIONAL DEVELOPMENT/EQUALIZATION —	
• "Establish a task force comprised of representatives of different industry sectors (high technology, tourism, value-added resources, etc.) and the venture capital community, boards of trade, chambers of commerce and other interested parties to develop more effective regional development agencies." • "Reform" regional development programs, including placing a much higher emphasis on reform to attract more venture capital.	• End "corporate welfare" and "regional handouts". • Put an end to the "alphabet soup of agencies like ACOA, CED-Q, FEDNOR, and WED." • "Maintain a strong equalization program to ensure that Canadians in all regions have access to vital services."

PC PARTY	CANADIAN ALLIANCE
— REGIONAL DEVELOPMENT/EQUALIZATION —	
• Bring in a two-year Community Investment Pilot Program for seasonal communities with very high unemployment rates. • "Revisit, with the provinces, the current equalization agreements to introduce a five-year break on the reduction of equalization benefits which currently occurs, and provide a review to ensure that new sources of revenue result in an improved economic climate."	
— FISHERIES/SHIPBUILDING —	
• "Manage the fisheries with the goal of conservation." • "Transfer the policy and science branches of Fisheries and Oceans to the east and west coasts to better understand and respond to the concerns of fishers." • Protect trans-boundary fisheries from unsustainable harvesting practices on our east and west coasts. • Invest more in fisheries science and research. • "Negotiate with the provinces a cost-shared Commercial Fisheries Infrastructure Program to ensure fisheries infrastructure, such as wharves, is constructed and maintained." • Exclude Canadian-built ships from Revenue Canada Leasing Rules. • Consider guaranteeing private sector debt financing for shipbuilding.	• Conservation must be the primary goal of Canada's fisheries policy. • Decentralize decision making in the Department of Fisheries and Oceans, and allow for greater input by fishermen and other stakeholders.

PC PARTY	CANADIAN ALLIANCE
— FISHERIES/SHIPBUILDING —	
• Refundable tax credit to Canadian ship owners or shipbuilders who contract to build a ship or contract for a conversion or major refit in a Canadian shipyard. • Officially support the sealing industry of Eastern and Northern Canada.	
— EDUCATION —	
• Bring in an income contingent loan repayment program for university graduates. • Implement an income tax credit based on the repayment of Canada Student Loan loan principal, "to a maximum of 10 per cent of the principal, per year, for the first ten years after graduation, provided the individual remains in Canada." • Eliminate the taxable status of scholarships. • "Establish the Canadian Institute for Learning and Technology, a new national centre of expertise and applied research in the use of technology for learning and teaching, spanning the school, college and university and lifelong learning sectors." • "Establish the E-campus Collaborations Program to support national collaborations amongst universities to co-develop courses and programs which are enabled by new learning technologies." • "Establish the Canadian E-learning Resource Library to provide the infrastructure for a nationwide exchange of E-learning content."	• Bring in an income contingent loan repayment program for university graduates. • Bring forward tax reform measures for parents who send their children to independent schools, while respecting provincial jurisdiction.

PC PARTY	CANADIAN ALLIANCE
— THE ENVIRONMENT —	

PC PARTY

- "Review existing environmental policies that affect human health and ensure there are measures to adequately protect all Canadians by assessing health risks to the most vulnerable – children and the elderly."

- Introduce a "Safe Water Act" to safeguard drinking water as well as enshrine Health Canada's guidelines for drinking water into law.

- "Introduce a Safe Air Act legislating acceptable air quality standards for Canadians that would be harmonized with the provinces and territories."

- "Achieve sector-by-sector agreements with industry to set targets to reduce emissions of various types of pollutants that are considered risks to the human health of our most vulnerable populations."

- Enact legislation to protect endangered species and encourage green power.

- Introduce incentives for using renewable sources of energy.

- "Table new pesticide legislation that would modernize the existing 30 year-old legislation."

CANADIAN ALLIANCE

- "Protect endangered species through community-based stewardship programs and stakeholder consensus."

- "Encourage business and industry to develop conservation solutions."

- "Work with the provinces in setting national standards and negotiating international agreements", and "back up standards with vigorous enforcement and meaningful penalties."

PC PARTY	CANADIAN ALLIANCE
— CROWN CORPORATIONS/CAPITAL INVESTMENTS —	

PC PARTY	CANADIAN ALLIANCE
• Open up the Canadian rail system to competition by and between all competent railway operators to create a more competitive and efficient rail transportation system that will benefit Canadian farmers.	• Privatize VIA rail.
• Make the CBC's mission and role as public broadcaster relevant to all regions of Canada.	• Sell off the federal government's remaining 20% stake in Petro-Canada.
• Rebuild Canada's crumbling highway system.	• "Allow CBC television and internet services to raise private capital while ensuring majority Canadian ownership and retaining a public CBC radio (including Radio Canada International)."
• Broaden and enhance the Airport Capital Assistance Program (ACAP) to ensure community airports are sustainable.	• Establish a National Highway Policy in partnership with the provinces to ensure the long-term viability of our national highways.
• Provide an adequate level of service with respect to the Marine Atlantic ferry service as specified in Term 32 of the Terms of Union of Newfoundland and Canada.	

— AGRICULTURE/FARMING —	
• Create the "Federal Agriculture Stabilization Transfer (FAST), a comprehensive national safety net program comprised of a revenue/income stabilization component and a reliable disaster relief fund".	• "Support safety net programs, including emergency disaster relief, crop insurance, and NISA (Net Income Stabilization Account), to assist farmers struggling against conditions outside their control."
• "Make membership in the Canadian Wheat Board a matter of discretion of the producer subject to the conduct of a free vote of all current members of the CWB to determine the powers of the CWB for the ensuing five years."	• "Give grain farmers freedom to make their own marketing choices, including through the Canadian Wheat Board."
	• "Will continue to support supply-managed farmers by reducing tariffs and changing domestic policies only when other countries match our commitments and provide guaranteed access to foreign markets."

PC PARTY	CANADIAN ALLIANCE
— AGRICULTURE/FARMING —	
• All possible steps must be taken by both federal and provincial governments to preserve the supply management system while recognizing that change within the system is necessary.	• "Launch an aggressive campaign through the WTO and NAFTA to reduce foreign subsidies."
• Support the development of a commercial and contractual grain handling system.	
• "Initiate a two-year horticultural pilot project to develop an agriculture/horticulture T-4 form that would enable Canadians to earn a certain amount tax-free when employed seasonally in the agriculture/horticultural sector."	
• Increase funding for investment in basic research, applied research and education.	
• "Pursue with the WTO a level playing field in resource industries, especially agriculture, to reduce government subsidies to these industries in other countries, so that there can be true free trade relating to resource based products."	

PC PARTY	CANADIAN ALLIANCE
— NATIVE ISSUES —	
• Endorses "inherent right" to Aboriginal self-government.	• "Respect existing aboriginal and treaty rights while helping aboriginal peoples participate fully in the mainstream of Canadian social and economic life."
• Give "Aboriginal people the power to raise their own revenues to help reduce the cycle of dependency."	
• Reform the Indian Act to make it less paternalistic.	• Make cuts to the Department of Indian Affairs and Northern Development.
• Government must respond "more energetically" to settle outstanding land and other claims.	• Ensure direct private ownership of native land and resources and remove their exemption from taxation.
• Phase out the "northern development" division from the Ministry of Indian Affairs and Northern Development and transfer those responsibilities to the territorial governments.	• "Settling unresolved land claims must be a high priority for the federal government."
— DEFENCE —	
• Supports "immediate additional annual funding for the next five years to maintain current capabilities and implement proposed long-term capital programs."	• Spend an additional $2 billion per year on national defence.
• Purchase modern, effective maritime helicopters.	• Recognizes the issues of "poor equipment, stretched personnel, low pay and low morale" must be addressed.
• Supports "the need to provide financial support to allow adequate levels of pay, medical and other benefits, including housing allowances (where necessary) as well as provision of adequate leaves away from station or theatre".	

PC PARTY	CANADIAN ALLIANCE
— DEFENCE —	

PC PARTY	CANADIAN ALLIANCE
• Implement a Veterans' Bill of Rights, and "conduct a review of the veterans' hospital to ensure that the needs of veterans are being met". • Establish an independent Inspector General position within the Department of National Defence. • "Establish a land base in British Columbia to provide assistance to the civil power in the event of natural disasters such as earthquakes, storms, etc."	

— PARLIAMENTARY/POLITICAL REFORM —

PC PARTY	CANADIAN ALLIANCE
• Reforms would consist of: more free votes, constitutional reform of the Senate under the general formula (seven provinces representing 50 per cent of the population plus the federal government) to elect senators, "re-balancing the constitutional powers of the Senate to reflect the objective of provincial, territorial and regional representation in the federal legislative process and ensuring the supremacy of the House of Commons on issues to avoid deadlock and political instability" and would ensure "distribution of seats on an equal basis determined through discussion with the provinces and territories". • Make the Ethics Commissioner report to Parliament and force MPs to benefit from pay raises only after an election is held.	• Reforms include free votes in the House of Commons, measures to "allow Canadians to bring forward citizen-initiated referendums to put their priorities on the national agenda through a Canada-wide vote"*, recall of MPs, election of Senators (appointing those who have been directly elected in their home province/territory "as a first step toward having an effective Senate elected on an equal basis," more parliamentary review of government appointments and fixed election dates every four years. *Note that the Canadian Alliance Declaration of Policy approved by the founding convention in January 2000 had referred to "binding referenda". The word "binding" was not in the November 2000 election platform.

PC PARTY	CANADIAN ALLIANCE
— IMMIGRATION —	
• "Focus immigration on those applicants who by educational backgrounds and job skills are needed in the country and are most likely to contribute to the development of Canadian society." • Continue to accept our "fair share" of refugees. • Speed the process for foreign students who are studying or have studied in Canada to apply for landed immigrant status.	• Maintain the current level of immigration, make it easier for immigrants who possess advanced skills and training to enter Canada, and "make the family reunification process truly responsive".
— FOREIGN POLICY AND INTERNATIONAL AID —	
• "Ensure that official development assistance encourages countries to become and remain self-sufficient." • "Integrate Canada's international relations, trade and international development policies so that they bring together the country's economic interests while promoting human rights and individual freedom."	• Replace CIDA with a "new agency at arm's length from government, with development and relief organizations directly represented on its board." • "Balance compassion and humanitarian concern with a commitment to advancing Canada's economic interests and protecting the defence and security of Canada and its allies."
— OTHER ISSUES —	
• Develop a National Homelessness Strategy "which would include a comprehensive range of measures aimed at preventing and alleviating homelessness in Canada". • Eliminate "inter-provincial trade barriers in commerce, labour, and capital mobility through non-constitutional means" and create an Inter-Provincial Trade Commission to oversee and carry out inter-provincial trade policies.	• Encourage counselling in any uncontested divorce where there are children involved, and ensure that "shared parenting" is the norm after divorce. • Protect marriage as "the exclusive union of one man and one woman". • "Use Ottawa's constitutional power to regulate trade to reduce provincial trade restrictions so that all goods, services, investments and economic activity will be subject to the same rules across the country."

PC PARTY	CANADIAN ALLIANCE
— OTHER ISSUES —	

PC PARTY	CANADIAN ALLIANCE
• Expand the list of medical expense claims for people with disabilities who are working. • Redirect resources from within the existing budget of Human Resources Development Canada to process the current backlog of Canada Pension Plan disability applications. • Commit to a Canadian "social audit" to be conducted by an arm's length agency similar to the Auditor General, the Privacy Commissioner and the Information Commissioner, to assess the effectiveness of federal spending on social programs. • Create a Minister of State for Seniors. • "Would not raise CPP contribution rates beyond levels adequate to ensure the long-term viability of the Plan." • "Work with the provinces to develop a comprehensive privacy and security code for electronic communications."	• Repeal preferential hiring laws. • Appoint a Chief Scientist for Canada to coordinate science activities in all government departments. • Promote choice and competition in the airline industry. • "Treat all Canadians equally, giving everyone the respect and dignity they deserve under the law." • "Respect the legitimate jurisdictions of Canada's provinces, including Quebec, so that they will have the tools they need to create the lasting prosperity and strong communities that Canadians desire."

WHY THE CANADIAN ALLIANCE AND THE PROGRESSIVE CONSERVATIVES SHOULD COMBINE FORCES

There are a number of convincing reasons for the Tories and the Alliance to unite. The first and most compelling is that Canada's national interest requires it. Most thinking Canadians are fed up with the spectacle of our two main opposition parties battling each other to a useless stalemate, each crowing over its own insignificant little victories and gloating over the other's temporary reverses, while the great Liberal steamroller crushes them both, and remains unscathed. It is partly the childish inability of these two conservative parties to cooperate that drove so many voters, especially in Ontario, to boycott the 2000 election. Canadians want, and need, a single, viable, credible conservative party that will once again offer a realistic alternative to perpetual Liberal rule, and in the meantime will be truly effective in holding an arrogant Liberal government to account. "Why can't you people get your act together?" has become the most frequently asked question by ordinary voters of activists from either party. All Canadians instinctively feel uncomfortable with permanent one-party government, but only active members of the two opposition parties are actually in a position to do something about it. We owe this step to our fellow citizens.

A second reason, equally cogent, is that the leaders, MPs and members of the two parties will never have the opportunity to implement any of their programs in government unless they combine their forces to get there. It is certainly true that the fiscal proposals of the Reform party have already had a huge impact on Liberal policy, and for that the party is to be congratulated. But the vicarious and grudging pleasure of watching your victorious adversary steal your best ideas hardly compares with the satisfaction of implementing them yourself from the government benches and the cabinet room.

Members of both parties must understand that nothing short of complete cooperation will work. For three elections, for eight years, each party has predicted the imminent collapse and disintegration of the other, and its own absorption of the other's support. It hasn't happened, and it won't happen for a very long time. If ever a situation cried out for applying the adage, "If you can't beat 'em, join 'em", it is this one. Those who believe that the current problems of the Alliance will drive all its supporters into the arms of the Tories in the next election are dreaming, just as were those who thought a year earlier that the reverse fate would befall the Tories. It is instructive to note that the Alliance drop in the polls since the 2000 election has benefitted the Liberals as much as the Tories. It is also instructive to consider that Social Credit, an earlier western-based party, elected western MPs continuously from 1935 to 1968 — with, it is true, the support of two provincial parties. The process of re-absorption of Social Credit supporters by the federal Tory and Liberal parties was long and gradual, taking 33 years — and that was in a time when those voters had a choice of two real national parties to go back to, as compared to only one today. Tory zealots should also remember that PC polling numbers have often risen between elections before, only to evaporate on election day.

Neither party can supplant the other, and neither party can win without the other. Happily, the electoral fit of the two parties is almost perfect. All of the Alliance's 66 seats are west of the Ottawa River, while ten of the Tories' 12 seats are east of it. The only provinces in which both parties hold seats are Manitoba and Alberta. It is perfectly conceivable, even highly likely, that all 78 sitting MPs of both parties would be re-elected if they were to run in the next election under a common banner — and this is even more likely if they were to negotiate an electoral pact. But this is just the tip of the iceberg. As mentioned in Chapter 1, there were 34 ridings won by Liberals in the 2000 election in which the combined Tory/Alliance vote would have taken the seat, and two more such ridings won by the NDP, enough to have raised a combined conservative opposition caucus to 114 members, reducing the Liberals to a minority with 138 seats. This would have reduced the difference between the two parties to only 24 seats instead of the present gap of 106 seats between the Liberals and the Alliance. Moreover, it is virtually certain that a return to a single nationwide conservative opposition party would attract a number of new supporters — conservative-minded Canadians who have either been voting Liberal by default or have been too disenchanted by all parties to vote at all. Even a small swing from the Liberals to a combined Conservative/Alliance party would be enough to give the combined party more seats than the Liberals — in 2000, the Liberals took 40.8% of the vote nationwide, whereas the combined total of the Alliance and the Tories was 37.7%, only three points behind.

The arguments for the Alliance and the Tories to combine in some fashion are both overwhelming and incontrovertible. The often-heard objection that most Tories would rather vote Liberal than Alliance, or that most Alliance supporters would never vote Conservative, is a complete red herring. The whole point of combining the two parties is precisely that neither group will ever be asked to vote for the other, but rather that both groups will be asked to support a new party combining the best elements of each, which members of both existing parties will have worked together to create. The challenge now is to stop inventing reasons why it can never be done, and to get on with the job for the good of Canada.

The doubters and the hesitant among us should consider the galvanizing words of Rabbi Hillel over eight centuries ago: *If not now, when?* To the rabbi's challenge we would add: *And if not this, what? And if not us, who?*

CHAPTER FOUR

Obstacles to Unity: the Failure of Leadership is Keeping the Two Parties Apart

In view of the overwhelming logic of bringing the Tories and the Alliance together, what is keeping them apart? There is an embarrassingly simple answer to this simple question: their leadership. It is not only that the leaders are failing to do the job, but even worse, they are often frustrating, both by action and inaction, the attempts and desires of others to bring the two parties together. And the governing councils and members of the two parties, not to mention the media, have so far been letting the leaders get away with it.

THE PARTY LEADERS

It is worth analyzing the interests and motives of the various players in this drama, which is both tragedy and farce. First, the leaders themselves. It is evident that the primary concern of each leader, although perhaps to different degrees, is to keep his job, which requires the preservation of his party and his position. It is easy to cloak personal ambition in the banner of one's sacred duty to one's great party or to the mythical "grassroots", the need to keep the other barbarians from the gates, and the inevitability of ultimate victory. And it must be admitted that, if you are a lifelong politician, the two leaders' jobs are very good jobs indeed, perhaps the best you might ever hope to have. The pay and the perks are excellent, the media attention and the deference of others very gratifying, ensuring that the oversize ego that seems to be a requisite of political leadership in Canada is always well fed and watered. What's more, your family, and the palace guard of your closest supporters (all appointed by you and dependent on your survival to keep their jobs), ceaselessly murmur in your ear that you are doing the right thing, that you must beware the base motives and perfidy of the other side, and that your party and your country need you, even if they don't all seem to realize this all the time. There is also the fear of appearing weak, of being accused of betraying your principles, or of leading your party into oblivion. What appears to be missing is any recognition of the overriding national and political interest, or any willingness to sacrifice personal or partisan considerations for the greater good.

To whom are the Alliance and PC leaders accountable? In the strict sense, to nobody except the party membership that elected them, in a process where every person who bought a membership had a vote. They are not formally accountable to their caucus, nor to the national governing body of their party. And even their party membership has no formal way of holding each leader accountable except in a general meeting, infrequently held. The Canadian Alliance has scheduled a general meeting for the first weekend of April 2002 in Edmonton. At the time of writing, the Progressive Conservatives have talked of a possible general meeting in August 2002, perhaps in Edmonton as well; their last such meeting was held in October 1999, shortly after Joe Clark was elected leader. So in practice, the party leaders are free to do exactly as they choose from one general meeting to the next, and they have traditionally used every means at their disposal to ensure that these rare general meetings reconfirm their leadership.

But even though the leaders cannot be forced to do the right thing, they cannot prevent *others* from doing it, provided these others are sufficiently determined. (An instructive precedent is Dalton Camp's successful crusade, as national president of the Progressive Conservative Association of Canada in the 1960s, to bring about a democratic review of the leadership of John Diefenbaker.) The "others", in this case, are the MPs of each party, the governing councils of each party, and ultimately the members of each party.

THE MEMBERS OF PARLIAMENT

Let's start with the MPs. In most cases, their primary concern is to get re-elected. If they think that their re-election will be best served by having no truck nor trade with the other party, this consideration will figure strongly in their actions. For example, given the extremely negative image in Atlantic Canada of the Reform party, with the Canadian Alliance not faring much better, the Atlantic MPs of the Progressive Conservative party have until recently taken pains to avoid any public association with either Reform or the Alliance — convinced that it would be the kiss of death electorally, no matter what its merits might otherwise be. Similarly, many Alliance MPs are petrified of being thought to be too friendly with the party of the hated Brian Mulroney, on whose back the Reform party was originally built. The only effective motivation for an MP of either party to support unification with the other is the hope that it might help get them onto the government side of the House. Strange to say, it seems that a number of MPs in both parties find this an insufficient reason for coming together, perhaps on the short-sighted theory that a bird in the hand (their seat in opposition) is worth two in the bush (their seat in government and a possible government post). Whatever the reason, there has been little sign of real leadership on this question from either caucus. While productive contacts have occurred between individual members of both caucuses, and meetings between the PC establishment and the so-called Democratic Representative Caucus of breakaway Alliance MPs, this is not nearly enough.

If caucus members find themselves in fundamental disagreement with the party leader, it is true that they do have one very effective weapon with which to resolve the dispute. Although the caucus cannot fire the leader, it can abandon him. Any MP can resign from the party caucus at any time, and either join another caucus or sit as an independent. This is how the Bloc Québécois began, with six dissident Conservatives being joined by two dissident Liberals in 1990. Three years later, the Bloc had become the Official Opposition. In theory, every Alliance or Tory MP could resign from the party caucus en masse, leaving the recalcitrant leader as leader of a caucus of one, himself. But this is a dangerous weapon to use, as it means abandoning the party label under which you were last elected, and risking defeat if your old party proves stronger than your new one in the ensuing election. In the present situation, the formation of a new caucus in the House, presumably with a view to forming a new party designed to bring together both Tory and Alliance supporters under a new leader, could succeed only if it attracted members from both the present Conservative and Alliance caucuses. Otherwise it is nothing more than a dissident group of Alliance MPs who are merely disgruntled with their own leader, instead of being motivated primarily by the larger issue of uniting the two parties for the good of the country.

THE PARTY GOVERNING COUNCILS

What of the governing bodies of the two parties? Constitutionally, these two bodies have the primary responsibility to decide whether there should be cooperation and to what degree, and to manage any process that is undertaken. They are not subject to the direction of either the leader or the caucus, although both of the latter have a degree of moral authority — more so in the case of the Tories. If the two national councils were to agree on a course of action, nothing could stop them, although any major initiatives would have to be ratified by the general membership of each party. In the case of the Canadian Alliance, on May 26, 2001, their national council unanimously instructed its then co-presidents to make a formal approach to their Conservative counterpart, and also asked its constituency associations throughout the country to make contact with the local PC association, in each case with a view to bringing the two parties closer together. The Tories started a consultation process with their own membership some time earlier, to gauge the level of interest in cooperating with the Alliance. So although too timidly and slowly, both governing bodies are moving tentatively in the right direction, with the Alliance once again out ahead.

The interests of national council or management committee members are of a different nature from those of the leaders and the MPs. In the first place, council members are virtually all volunteers, and their day jobs and careers do not depend on their political decisions. Secondly, they have a fiduciary and legal responsibility, in a way that the leader and MPs do not, to manage the affairs of the party in the best interests of its members. Thirdly, they, not the leader or the MPs, are ultimately responsible for raising the money necessary to keep the party functioning, for staffing the party office, for establishing and recognizing party associations in the ridings and elsewhere, and for recruiting, approving and denying party memberships and parliamentary candidacies. They are fully conscious that the party is bigger and more important than any leader or MP, and that sometimes the interests of the party as a whole may differ from those of the leader or members of the caucus. Members of both party councils, as stewards for the party above all, should realize that this is one of those times, and they should summon up the courage and the independence to fulfil their constitutional and fiduciary responsibilities

THE PARTY MEMBERS

Finally, the general membership itself — the "ordinary Canadians" who are motivated to buy a party membership every year, to maintain the constituency associations, to contribute money, and to work at elections. The first thing to remember is that this membership is constantly changing, and that it can fluctuate drastically from year to year. One effect of this fluidity is the natural tendency, when things are not going well for a party, for many members to vote with their feet, either by resigning or by simply not renewing their annual membership. The consequence of this shrinkage is that only the diehards tend to remain, and they are the ones least likely to approve of any form of compromise. So often, the more desperate a party is, the smaller its membership becomes, yet the more they tend to dig in, deny reality, and elevate the mere blind survival of the institution above any higher purpose such as winning elections or forming a government. Keeping the party alive becomes an end in itself.

This being said, both of the opposing leaders whom each party originally loved to hate have now gone, thereby removing much of the motivation or excuse for their mutual hostility. The Reform party was formed largely by western Canadians who disliked the policies of Brian Mulroney, while the remaining members of the Progressive Conservative party after 1993 tended to blame Preston Manning for destroying their historic party west of Quebec. Canadian Alliance members, on the other hand, have much less reason to hate Albertan Joe Clark, while Tories have no particular reason to hate the current Alliance leadership. It is probably the case today that a strong majority of the membership of both parties is in favour of a reconciliation of some sort, provided that the basic principles and interests of both parties can be respected.

It is sometimes claimed by media commentators and the occasional individual party member that there are fundamental differences in policy and culture between the two parties that are absolutely irreconcilable. This is nonsense. As we saw in the comparison of the 2000 election platforms of the two parties in Chapter 3, the actual policy differences are few and relatively minor. Both parties are democratic, conservative and open to all Canadians. Of course it is a simple matter to find instances of unacceptable statements made by a few party members — as with any party, including the Liberals — and to claim that they represent the entire party through guilt by association. But this is just a stratagem to obscure more selfish and ignoble motives in refusing to contemplate any rapprochement. The fact is that where there's a will, there's a way. All that is needed to bring our two parties together is some surviving shred, if any can be found in today's leaders, of the magnificent display of political will shown by the Fathers of Confederation in bringing their four provinces together to form our country in the first place.

TWO PARTISAN ELEMENTS WITHOUT LEGITIMACY: UNELECTED SENATORS, AND PAID STAFF

There are at present 30 Progressive Conservative senators, one Canadian Alliance senator (former Tory party president Gerry St.

Germain), and five independent senators — in addition to the 57 Liberal senators. (There are also 12 vacancies.) These men and women are in patronage heaven, having all been appointed to their positions without the inconvenience of having to get elected, and enjoying the luxury of a taxpayer-funded sinecure until the age of 75 (followed by a generous pension) — again with no obligation ever to submit themselves to the judgment of the electorate (which pays their salaries), or to that of anybody else.

These parliamentarians are unique in that they are accountable to absolutely nobody — except, in the most blatant cases of misconduct, to the other senators. But particularly in the case of the Progressive Conservative party, they have extraordinary influence. This arises partly from the fact that in the Tory caucus, the unelected senators outnumber the 12 elected MPs by a ratio of five to two. But it also comes from the happenstance that a handful of the Tory senators are useful to party leader Joe Clark in his strategy of resisting any deal with the Canadian Alliance. In his charade of pretending to be cooperative with the Alliance by sitting down with the small faction of Alliance dissidents at Mont Tremblant in August, 2001, Mr. Clark took care to surround himself with such hard-liners as senators Norman Atkins and Marjory LeBreton. He pointedly excluded the many other Tory senators who strongly favour true cooperation with the Alliance.

The fact is that, whichever side they are on, these people represent nobody but themselves. Since they have no need to run for election, they have no need to keep in touch with or speak for the mainstream of conservative opinion in Canada. They can indulge themselves in the unreality of dreams of past glories, and in the illusion that their party is still the powerful national institution it was before 1993. After all, it is of no material concern to them whether the Liberals are ever defeated or not. Their cozy little world is just fine as it is, thank you. Tory senators should be disqualified from any participation in talks with the Alliance on the grounds, not of conflict of interest, but of total absence of interest and of any democratic legitimacy.

Paid party employees and parliamentary staffers, on the other hand, do have a clear conflict of interest on the issue of possible unification of the Alliance and the Tories: some of them might lose their jobs in a unified party. Small wonder that Tory staffers (and even some Alliance staffers) are a main source of opposition to official talks between the two parties.

CHAPTER FIVE

The Benefit to Liberals of a Divided Opposition

How the Rivalry Between Tories and Reform/Alliance Keeps the Liberals in Power

There have been three major benefits to the Liberal party arising directly from the split between the Conservatives and Reform/Alliance since 1993. The first is the simple mathematical effect of having two parties dividing the votes that formerly went to a single party. The second is the dramatic drop in voter turnout, particularly in Ontario, which has cut disproportionately into the "conservative" vote. And the third is the damaging effect on the conservative cause of dividing scarce electoral resources between two warring parties, instead of concentrating them in a single party battling only the Liberals.

1) Facing two conservative parties, the Liberals win many more unearned seats than if facing only one

First, the Liberals have won a significant number of seats in each of the last three elections because opposing votes were split between two conservative parties, instead of all going to a single conservative party as was generally the case before 1993. Owing to this "vote-splitting", in 1993 the Liberals took 43 seats they would not otherwise have won; in 1997, 38 seats, and in 2000, 34 seats. It is worth noting that the NDP also benefitted from the same phenomenon, although to a much lesser degree, winning four seats through conservative vote-splitting in 1993, four in 1997, and two in 2000. If one assumes that a single conservative party (call it the United conservatives) had taken all the votes cast for the Tories, Reform and the Alliance in all these seats, the results of the three elections would have been quite different. Borrowing an accounting term and calling this electoral recalculation a "normalized" election, the actual as compared to the normalized results are as follows:

Actual vs. "normalized" seat results for Canada, federal elections 1993-2000

	1993 Actual	1993 Normalized	1997 Actual	1997 Normalized	2000 Actual	2000 Normalized
Liberal	177	134	155	117	172	138
NDP	9	5	21	17	13	11
Bloc Québécois	54	54	44	44	38	38
Reform/Alliance	**52**	—	**60**	—	**66**	—
PC	**2**	—	**20**	—	**12**	—
Other	1	1	1	1	—	—
United conservatives	—	**101**	—	**122**	—	**114**
TOTAL	295	295	301	301	301	301

This analysis shows that in 2000, a United conservative party would have won 36 more seats than did the Alliance and the Tories independently (114 seats instead of just 78); 25 of these 36 seats are in Ontario, where the United conservative total would therefore have risen to 27 seats, including the two seats actually won by the Alliance. Note that the Liberals would have been reduced to a minority in both the 1993 and 2000 elections, while the United conservatives would have had the most seats in 1997 and would probably have formed the government.

The argument is often made that one should not assume that all the votes cast for Tories and Reform/Alliance *would* in fact have gone to a single United conservative candidate. This argument is based largely on a survey of only 417 Progressive Conservative voters made for the 1997 Canadian Election Study. This study was conducted by four Canadian political scientists: Neil Nevitte of the University of Toronto, Elisabeth Gidengil of McGill University, and André Blais and Richard Nadeau, both of Université de Montréal. The survey they commissioned found that 45.8% of the 417 PC voters surveyed reported the Liberal party as their second choice, while 15.3% reported the NDP and only 12.7% Reform. The margin of error was not reported. In considering the huge weight and importance given ever since to this single survey by opponents of Preston Manning's United Alternative movement to bring Reformers and Tories together in a new party, one is reminded of British statesman Benjamin Disraeli's conclusion that there are three kinds of lies: lies, damned lies, and statistics. In fact, after examining the raw data, the purported conclusions of this study cannot withstand even the most cursory scrutiny or analysis — which, of course, none of our credulous journalists ever bothered to perform.

Even without questioning the statistical validity of so small a sample, or the representativeness and method of selection of voters willing to respond to such questions, or the rate of response, or the influence on Tory respondents of the constant contemporary vilification of Reform by Tory leader Jean Charest, let us begin by noting that 70 of these PC voters were in the Atlantic provinces, where Reform was largely unknown in 1997, and 124 of them were in Quebec, where Preston Manning had been terminally demonized by both the French and English media as a unilingual western anti-Quebecer. This means that 46.5% of the total sample (194 respondents out of 417) could be virtually *guaranteed* to say that they would not vote for Reform. What is surprising is that only 22 of the 70 Atlantic Tories (31%) cited the Liberals as their second choice, while 35 of them (50%) chose the NDP. Predictably, out of the 194 respondents east of Ontario, a grand total of *four* gave Reform as their second choice (three in New Brunswick and one in Nova Scotia). Of the 124 Quebec Tories surveyed, 62 (50%) chose the Liberals and 42 (34%) the Bloc Québécois. For some reason, one PC voter in Quebec firmly gave the PCs as his or her second choice as well — but as one would expect, none cited Reform.

West of Quebec, on the other hand, where the sample of Tory voters was 223, a total of 49 respondents said they would vote Reform as their second choice, or 22%. Of the 74 Tory voters surveyed in the four western provinces, 22 gave Reform as their second choice (30%), and 29 the Liberal party (39%). All this notorious survey really demonstrates is that if they had been obliged to vote for another party in 1997, many Tories would understandably have chosen the devil they knew over the devil they didn't know.

Arguments which cite this poll as conclusive evidence that unification is either impossible or useless are fundamentally specious and diversionary red herrings. The blatantly obvious point that these arguments (intentionally) miss is that if a unified conservative party existed, no Tory voters would be asked to vote for either Reform or the Canadian Alliance, just as no Alliance supporters would be asked to vote Tory. Rather, both would be asked to vote for an entirely new conservative party, with new leadership, which ideally would have shed the elements that apparently repel some conservatives from each of the existing conservative parties. The most convincing refutation of these red herrings is the fact that when they had the chance, none of these voters actually did vote Liberal, so there are no grounds for assuming that they would do so if a more attractive first choice were available to them. Indeed a far stronger case can be made that a united conservative party would attract not fewer but more voters than the sum of actual PC and Reform/Alliance supporters. The fact is that most diehard Tory voters do not give much thought to a second choice, since they do not have to make one. Strong partisans (like the PC respondent in Quebec) may even say there is no such thing: as between heaven and hell, what indeed is your second choice? And east of Manitoba especially, the Liberals are the old devil that Tories know, while Reform was the new devil they didn't know.

Some commentators have also observed that even if all the votes cast recently for the two existing parties *could* somehow be combined into a single conservative party, these votes still would not be enough to defeat the Liberals. They then seem to throw up their hands, concluding that the whole exercise is pointless. But there is indeed a point, which they again choose to miss. The point is that the Liberals benefit from a second, extremely important, although less self-evident advantage from the ongoing rivalry between the Tories and the Reform/Alliance party that has raged unabated since Reform was founded by Preston Manning in 1987 — almost 15 years ago. This advantage is the subject of the next two sections.

2) The internecine war among conservatives has driven voters away, and has also contributed to the huge drop in voter turnout in Ontario since 1993

This second benefit to the Liberals might be called the turnoff factor, or the plague-on-both-your-houses factor, that has driven many previous conservative voters away from both parties in confusion and disgust in view of their childish failure to resolve their differences and reunite. While a number of these disillusioned conservatives, especially in Ontario, have reluctantly decided to vote Liberal for lack of an acceptable national alternative, a number have also found that there is no party that they could in all conscience vote for, and have simply stayed home and opted out of recent elections altogether.

There are two strong indications of the turnoff factor evident in Ontario for the last three elections. The first is the decline in the total conservative popular vote since 1988 and before, both in absolute numbers and as a percentage of valid votes cast. The second is the shocking decline in voter turnout over the same period.

First, the number of "conservative" votes cast in Ontario since 1984. The following table shows the actual number of votes cast for each "conservative" party, followed in each case by the percentage of total votes cast in the province. Then, for the three most recent elections, where the conservative vote was divided between two parties, it is added back together and shown as a notional overall "conservative" percentage of the popular vote. This shows that the "conservative" share of votes cast has not changed significantly since 1988, even though the actual number of such votes has been constantly declining. But this gives a very misleading picture of what has actually happened.

Underneath the table is another table showing the total number of Ontario registered voters, or electors, for each election. Beneath that number is another percentage, this time showing the "conservative" votes as a percentage, not of votes cast, but of *total registered voters*. The point is to indicate the constant erosion in both the number and the percentage of all Ontarians who have been prepared to vote "conservative", despite the constant increase in the size of the Ontario electorate during the period.

Total "conservative" votes cast (and "conservative" per cent of total votes cast) in federal elections in Ontario, 1984-2000

	1984	%	1988	%	1993	%	1997	%	2000	%
PC	2,113,187	47.6	1,788,116	38.2	859,596	17.6	871,616	18.8	642,438	14.4
Reform	—	—	—	—	913,691	20.1	886,787	19.1	—	—
CA	—	—	—	—	—	—	—	—	1,051,209	23.6
Total "cons."	2,113,187	47.6	1,788,116	38.2	1,777,407	37.7	1,758,403	37.9	1,693,647	38.0

Per cent of total *registered* Ontario electors who voted "conservative" federally, 1984-2000

	1984	1988	1993	1997	2000
Total Electors	5,882,320	6,309,375	7,266,097	7,115,785	7,713,744
% voting "cons."	35.9	28.3	24.4	24.7	22.0

The preceding table shows that the "conservative" side has suffered a net loss of almost 420,000 Ontario votes since 1984, or almost 20% of its 1984 total, during a period when Ontario's electorate has grown by 1,831,424 people, or 31%. While almost 36% of registered electors were prepared to vote for conservative candidates in 1984, only 22% were in 2000, a shrinkage of over two-fifths. Meanwhile, the total number of Liberal votes in Ontario has also declined since its peak of 2,383,065 in 1993, but less dramatically: to 2,294,593 in 1997, and to 2,292,075 in 2000. It is misleading to claim, as do some western observers, that Ontario is having a mad love affair with the Liberal party while rejecting all other suitors. The reality is that Ontario voters are disenchanted with all parties, although mostly with the conservative ones, and increasing numbers are simply not voting, as we will see next. (Note: the surprising drop in the total number of electors between 1993 and 1997 is due to the introduction before 1997 of the permanent voters list, which was initially less comprehensive than the former system of door-to-door enumeration.)

With regard to voter turnout in Ontario, the average turnout over the 17 elections from 1935 to 1988 was 75.5%, the fifth highest of all the provinces (trailing PEI at 84%, Saskatchewan at 79.1%, New Brunswick at 77.7% and Nova Scotia at 77.3%). In 1984 the Ontario turnout was 75.8%, and in 1988 it was 74.6%, right around the long-term average. But starting in 1993, Ontario voters have increasingly stayed home in droves. The turnout in 1993 dropped 6.9 points to 67.7%; in 1997 it dropped a further 2.1 points to 65.6%, and in 2000 the decline was precipitous, down 7.6 points to 58%. Over only three elections, after remaining stable for over fifty years, Ontario's voter turnout dropped by an incredible 16.6 points. This means that almost one quarter of those who always used to vote religiously in every federal election before 1993 failed to do so in 2000.

Such a huge decline in voter turnout over only eight years cannot be explained away by just the usual reasons — bad weather on voting day, lack of interest in politics, time constraints of daily life, etc. While less extreme declines have been observed elsewhere, there is only one credible explanation for such a radical change: a massive new indifference or even distaste among voters for all of the parties and politicians currently on offer has to be a contributing factor. This diagnosis is confirmed by the fact that the decline in turnout has reduced the vote of all parties in Ontario since 1988; but it is the "conservative" side that has suffered the greatest loss in support. There are three obvious reasons for this: (1) the division on the conservative side caused by the existence of two parties competing for the same pool of votes; (2) the failure of any of the leaders of these two parties (Campbell, Charest, and Clark for the

Tories; Manning and Day for Reform/Alliance) to favourably impress Ontario voters; and (3) the increasing use of negative advertising and image-making. Not surprisingly, the relentless character assassination of all the leaders by their opponents causes many Ontarians to react in disgust at the entire process, and to conclude that all recent conservative leaders are either incompetents, extremists, or except in the case of Charest, parochial westerners of no benefit or interest to Ontario.

3) Scarce electoral resources are divided between two conservative parties bent on mutual destruction

The third factor that has benefitted the Liberals in Ontario is the division between two conservative parties of the essential election resources of good candidates, money, volunteers — and especially strategic expertise and experience in directing a modern election campaign. Not only have the Tory and Reform/Alliance campaigns had to make do with a fraction of the resources that used to be available to a single party before 1993, but they have largely dissipated their campaign energies in fighting each other to a standstill instead of combining them against their true natural enemy, the Liberal party.

Both parties have been further weakened in Ontario by the effective neutralization of most of premier Mike Harris's experienced and successful provincial campaign team, who have largely sat out the last two federal elections, partly so as not to offend either the Tory component or the Reform/Alliance element of their provincial political coalition, and partly because of poor relations with the federal leaders (especially Charest and Clark on the PC side, and Day on the Alliance side). The failure to build strong relations with the most successful conservative party in Canada, in the province that has been the deciding factor in every recent election, must be laid squarely at the door of these three men.

Preston Manning at least made a serious effort, but in his only election when Harris was in office (1997), it was premature to expect the entire Harris organization to support Reform.

The effect of this dispersion and neutralization of essential but scarce resources has probably been most devastating at the level of the strategic direction and management of election campaigns. In 1997, Jean Charest lost confidence in his campaign team right at the beginning of the election, ditched his campaign plan at the last minute and turned everything over to his long-time strategist Jodi White, who was unable to mount an effective Ontario campaign in the brief time available, winning only one seat. Meanwhile, Reform made the miscalculation of running their notorious TV ads implying that Canada had had enough of political leaders from Quebec. While these ads may conceivably have firmed up Reform's support in some marginal western seats, they effectively destroyed its chances in Ontario, where most voters are more concerned about national unity. Reform lost its only Ontario seat.

In 2000, the Tories started at about 6 % in Ontario, handicapped by Joe Clark's image as a has-been trying a hopeless comeback. But thanks to a strong debate performance by Clark, and the effective use of scarce funds by campaign manager John Laschinger for some inventive anti-Chrétien TV ads, they improved their position to 14.4% on election day, helped immeasurably by a disastrous Alliance campaign. The Tories nevertheless failed to win a single Ontario seat. The ineptness of the Alliance campaign in Ontario in 2000 can be traced mainly to inexperienced strategic direction and management, and the lack of a qualified and battle-hardened general staff. The two Eastern Ontario Alliance victories were won by candidates who succeeded in distancing themselves from the national campaign and ran largely on local issues against vulnerable Liberal opponents.

It might be argued that there is a fourth benefit that the Liberal party has enjoyed from the presence of two parties to its political right. This has enabled the Liberals to position themselves as the only party of the moderate centre, the position preferred by the great majority of Canadian voters, while branding the Alliance in particular (their main rival) as a party of social conservatives completely out of step with mainstream Ontario opinion. It was never possible for the Liberals to successfully portray the federal Progressive Conservative party as extremist. On the other hand, the provincial Tories under Mike Harris have been strong fiscal conservatives, while remaining sufficiently moderate on controversial social issues to be acceptable to a plurality of Ontario voters. It is interesting to compare the recent federal elections (see the previous table) with the allocation of the popular vote and the voter turnout in the last five provincial elections in Ontario, where there has been only a single conservative party opposing the Liberals and the NDP. The provincial results are set out in the following table:

Total votes cast (and per cent) for each major party in Ontario provincial elections, 1985-1999

	1985 Winning Leader Miller (PC) minority	%	1987 Peterson (Lib.)	%	1990 Rae (NDP)	%	1995 Harris (PC)	%	1999 Harris (PC)	%
PC	1,343,044	36.9	931,473	24.7	944,564	23.5	1,870,110	44.8	1,978,059	45.1
Liberal	1,377,965	37.9	1,788,214	47.3	1,302,134	32.4	1,291,326	31.1	1,751,472	39.9
NDP	865,507	23.8	970,813	25.7	1,509,506	37.6	854,163	20.6	551,009	12.6
Total Votes Cast	3,635,699		3,777,311		4,018,079		4,158,370		4,390,207	
Total Electors	5,950,295		6,067,378		6,315,949		6,667,798		7,598,407	
% of electors voting PC	22.6		15.4		15.0		28.0		26.0	
Turnout	61.5		62.7		64.4		62.9		58.3	

This table shows that in 1995, Mike Harris's provincial PC party received 44.8% of the Ontario vote. Two years later, the combined federal vote of Reform and the federal PC party in Ontario was only 37.9%, almost seven points less. In 1999 Harris increased his vote share slightly to 45.1%, whereas in the 2000 federal election, the combined total of the Alliance and the PCs was again only 38%, about the same as in 1997. This was also seven critical percentage points less than the support given to conservative Mike Harris by the same electorate just 18 months earlier.

Surely it is not too great a leap of faith to conclude that a single federal conservative party, competently led, might aspire to a vote share of 45% in Ontario. If it can be done provincially, can it not be done federally? Indeed, Brian Mulroney received a 47.6% vote share in Ontario in 1984. It is patently untrue to claim that a strong plurality of Ontarians will never vote for a federal small-c conservative party, considering they have done just that provincially in the last two elections.

During his first term, Mike Harris reduced the number of provincial ridings in Ontario from 130 to 103, and made them congruent with the 103 federal ridings, giving them the same names as well. So a seat comparison between Mike Harris's 1999 victory and the 2000 federal results is particularly revealing, as it is now possible for the first time to compare provincial and federal results in Ontario simply and accurately.

In 1999, Mike Harris's Conservatives won 59 of Ontario's 103 provincial seats. As we know, in the 2000 federal election, only two conservative candidates won federal seats in Ontario — Scott Reid and Cheryl Gallant for the Alliance. We have already seen that the combined votes of PC and CA candidates would have won 27 ridings in Ontario in 2000, instead of two. Not surprisingly, 21 of these 27 ridings were also won by Mike Harris in 1999. But in 1999, because of his seven percentage points higher level of support, Harris won 38 Ontario ridings which a federal United conservative would still not have won in 2000. It is in these 38 ridings that one would also expect a united federal party to have the best prospects for additional wins. Conversely, and perhaps curiously, a federal United conservative would have taken six Ontario ridings in 2000 which Mike Harris did *not* take in 1999. These six ridings, mostly held by strong provincial Liberal incumbents, are Elgin-Middlesex-London, Hastings-Frontenac-Lennox and Addington, Renfrew-Nipissing-Pembroke, St. Catharines, Stormont-Dundas-Charlottenburgh, and Thunder Bay-Atikokan.

In conclusion, the Tory-Alliance rivalry, like the Tory-Reform rivalry before it, continues to yield huge unearned and undeserved benefits to the Liberals. But our analysis of these benefits shows clearly that if this rivalry were resolved, and if the Liberals had to face only a single united conservative party as before 1993, this party would immediately be competitive with the Liberal party. It would start with 78 sitting members, in every province but one, and would be in an excellent position to regain enough Ontario seats in the next election to reduce the Liberals to a minority at the very least, or to form its own minority or even majority government at best, as in 1984 and 1988.

CHAPTER SIX

GRITLOCK: The Inevitable Consequence of Continuing the Division

It should by now be clear to the reader that nothing short of a viable alternative, eventually in the form of a strong single national conservative party, can ever break the grip of the Liberal party on the federal government. But there are still some naïve or deluded souls who will argue passionately, against all evidence, that a formal reunification of the Tories and the Alliance is unnecessary, and that it is only a matter of weeks or months before one of the two parties collapses utterly and falls into the waiting arms of the other like an overripe fruit. In 2000, it was the Tories who were "on the verge of extinction", while in 2001, it has been the Alliance. Currently, it is mainly Tories who seem to think that the tide has irreversibly turned in their favour, and that they will somehow magically return to government in the next election, or at least to official opposition, without any need to sully their hands by talking to the Alliance, which will simply have vanished by then. Since these well-meaning dreamers have obviously not done their electoral homework, the following facts about the underlying regional strength of support for the two parties — and their opponents — should bring all but the completely innumerate to their senses.

1) In British Columbia, Alberta and Saskatchewan (74 seats), the Alliance has been unassailable at over 50% of the vote, the Tories barely alive; the Liberals, not the Tories, would benefit most from an Alliance decline

While it is true that with four parties in contention in an electoral system that was designed for two, the number of seats won by each party can vary widely from election to election depending on which of the four might squeak in first in close ridings, the underlying popular vote for each party is less volatile. Long-term trends in voting patterns are easily discernible, and it is possible to calculate fairly exactly the degree of "swing" in the popular vote (change from one party to another) that would be required for any given outcome of seats. Even if one assumes a swing from the Alliance to the Tories far greater than ever seen in any democracy, it still would not be enough to allow the Tories to completely replace the Alliance in British Columbia, Alberta or Saskatchewan.

On the other hand, the combined Tory-Alliance vote in these three provinces would have been sufficient in 2000 to take all but eight of their 74 seats (the Alliance now holds 60 of them). If we repeat for B.C., Alberta and Saskatchewan the same "normalization" analysis that we did for the whole country at the beginning of Chapter 5, these are the results:

Actual vs. "normalized" seat results for British Columbia, Alberta and Saskatchewan, federal elections 1993-2000

	1993		1997		2000	
	Actual	Normalized	Actual	Normalized	Actual	Normalized
Liberal	15	5	9	4	9	6
NDP	7	3	8	8	4	2
Reform/Alliance	**50**	—	**57**	—	**60**	—
PC	**0**	—	**0**	—	**1**	—
United conservatives	—	**64**	—	**62**	—	**66**
TOTAL	72	72	74	74	74	74

95

The popular vote in these three provinces has been overwhelmingly in favour of Reform/Alliance in the three elections since 1993. In B.C., their vote has grown from 36.4% to 43.1% to 49.9%. In Alberta, it has been even stronger, growing from 52.3% to 54.6% to 58.9%. In Saskatchewan, the growth has been most rapid of all, from 27.2%, to 36%, to 47.7%. Meanwhile, the Tory popular vote in B.C., which was 13.5% in 1993 under native daughter Kim Campbell, has declined to 6.2% in 1997 and 7.3% in 2000. In Alberta, the Tories took 14.6% of the vote in 1993, and 14.4% in 1997, declining to 13.5% in 2000 under native son Joe Clark. And in Saskatchewan, which has become the worst province in Canada for the Tories, their vote has slumped from 11.3% in 1993, to 7.8% in 1997, to a miserable 4.8% in 2000. The unvarnished truth is that in the last election, the Alliance beat the Tories by a crushing 42.6 points in B.C., 45.4 points in Alberta, and 42.9 points in Saskatchewan. For the Tories to completely replace the Alliance in these three provinces would require an unheard-of move of some 40% of all voters from one existing party to another between just two elections. This has never happened in Western Canada, and it simply will not happen. Even in the big 1993 swing to Reform away from an unpopular PC government, the Tories in B.C. dropped only 21 points from their previous 34.4% in 1988 to 13.5%; in Alberta they dropped 37 points, from 51.8% to 14.6%; and in Saskatchewan 25 points, from 36.4% to 11.3%.

A far more likely scenario, if the Alliance vote were to begin the slow and gradual decline over several elections that is typical of western protest parties, is that the main beneficiaries in terms of seats would be the Liberals. In British Columbia, the Liberal popular vote has stayed fairly steady through the last three elections, at 28.1%, 28.8%, and 27.7%. With the virtual wipe-out of the provincial NDP in the 2001 election, support for the federal

NDP, already in decline (from 18.2% in 1997 to 11.3% in 2000), can be expected to drop further, to the likely advantage of the Liberals. Even in Alberta, the Liberals have been well ahead of the Tories since 1993, at 25.1%, 24%, and 20.9%. Even though the NDP vote in Alberta is small (5.4% in 2000), Alberta Liberals should benefit somewhat from the ongoing national decline of the NDP (from 11% in 1997 to 8.5% in 2000). The Liberals have become weakest in Saskatchewan, mainly because of the continuing strength of the NDP, propped up by the provincial NDP government. The Liberal vote (32.1% in 1993, 24.7% in 1997, and 20.7% in 2000) will undoubtedly be strengthened by the current NDP decline both federally and provincially.

2) Only in Manitoba (14 seats), most electorally diverse of all the provinces, did all four parties win seats in 2000; the Liberals led, the Alliance was close behind, then the NDP, with the Tories a distant fourth

Manitoba, the geographic centre of the country, has also become a microcosm of the national political picture. Manitoba is the only province in which all four contending parties won seats in 1997 and 2000, and is the meeting point of the western-based Reform/Alliance and the eastern-based Tories. In 1993, Manitoba became the enduring eastern outpost of Reform, giving Preston Manning 22.4% of its votes but only one seat, while the Liberals took 12 seats with 45% of the vote; the NDP took the remaining seat with 16.7%. In 1997 the Tories established their western beachhead in Manitoba, winning a single seat and 17.8% of the vote. Reform gained two more seats in 1997 and increased its vote slightly to 23.7%, while the Liberal vote dropped significantly to 34.3%, good for only six seats; the NDP recovered to four seats with 23.2%. The Liberal decline and the Alliance growth continued in 2000, with the Liberals falling to five seats and 32.5%, and the Alliance rising to four seats and 30.4%. While the NDP and Conservative seat totals did not change, both parties lost vote share in 2000; the NDP vote dropped to 20.9%, and the Conservative vote to 14.5%. Manitoba appears to have discovered a reasonable approximation of proportional representation, giving each party more or less the number of seats warranted by its popular vote. Too bad that Ontario does not do likewise.

3) In Ontario (103 seats), the Liberals are unassailable at over 50% of the vote; as long as the Tories and the Alliance keep battling each other for a useless second place, the Liberals will sweep the province

In the last three elections in Ontario, the Liberal popular vote has been very consistent, at 52.9%, 49.5% and 51.5%. The problem is that Reform/Alliance and the Tories have also been fairly consistent, but each at well under half the Liberal total. The Reform/Alliance figures are 20.1%, 19.1%, and 23.6%, while the Tories have done rather worse at 17.6%, 18.8%, and 14.4% in 2000 — the great Joe Clark "revival". It should be clear to everyone by now that these two conservative parties could continue to fight it out for decades in Ontario without a final victory for either one. And meanwhile the Liberals, like Great Britain in the eighteenth-century heyday of the Balance of Power period in European affairs, and like Bill Davis in the 1970s when he won elections in Ontario with 40% of the vote against an evenly divided opposition, will do their utmost to prop up the weaker party to ensure that the other one doesn't get too strong. Joe Clark would have to lead his party, currently without a single seat in Ontario, to 40% in the polls (a gain of over 25 points from the 2000 election) before he could be taken seriously as an election-day contender against the 101 Liberal incumbents. With two conservative parties in the field, the likelihood of this happening is nil. And if the two parties do not come together before the next election, either Stockwell Day will have reversed his own party's slide in the polls, or he will have given way to a new leader of the Canadian Alliance who will be better equipped to do so. The inevitable result of this insane scenario, still advocated by some Ontario federal Tories, is continued stalemate on the right, with the Liberals continuing to laugh all the way to 24 Sussex Drive.

4) In Quebec (75 seats), the Liberals are successfully beating back the Bloc Québécois to recover their traditional supremacy; neither the Tories nor the Canadian Alliance are even distant contenders

After suffering their worst Quebec drubbing in history at the hands of Brian Mulroney in 1984 and 1988, and after seeing almost half of Quebec's voters rush into the arms of Lucien Bouchard in 1993, the Liberals have slowly but steadily been making an impressive comeback in the province ever since. Their percentage of the popular vote over the last six elections shows a dramatic plunge, followed by a gradual recovery toward their pre-Trudeau levels of 45%. The actual figures are 68.2% in 1980, Trudeau's final election and their six-decade high (against Joe Clark as Tory leader); followed by a drop of almost 33 points to 35.4% as Mulroney faced Turner for the first time in 1984; a further drop to 30.3% in 1988, their all-time low; then 33% against Bouchard's 49% in 1993; then 36.7% in 1997 against 38% for Gilles Duceppe; and back to 44.2% in 2000, as Chrétien finally succeeded in pulling ahead of the Bloc at 40% (although he still took two fewer seats than Duceppe).

Meanwhile, the figures for the Conservatives over the same six elections are almost the reverse, except that they have finished up well behind their pre-Trudeau levels of around 21%. The Tory percentages are 12.6% (Clark), 50.2% and 52.7% (Mulroney), 13.5% (Campbell), 22.2% (Charest), and finally a mere 5.6% (Clark again), by far their worst performance in history. In 2000, the Clark Tories were even beaten in Quebec by Stockwell Day's Canadian Alliance: running candidates throughout Quebec for the first time, the Alliance took 6.2% of the vote.

The message out of Quebec for both Tories and Alliance supporters is: (1) that the Liberals are only going to get stronger there; (2) that even united, the two conservative parties have little chance in Quebec unless they have a bilingual leader; (3) that if they ever want to form a Canadian government again, they had better begin cooperating outside Quebec; and (4) they had better do this sooner rather than later, while the Bloc Québécois still has the ability to keep some Quebec seats out of Liberal hands. All conservatives should remember that 100 Liberal seats in Ontario plus 52 Liberal seats in Quebec add up to a Liberal majority government, even if the Liberals do not win a single seat in any other province or territory.

5) In the Atlantic region (32 seats), the Liberals dominate, the Alliance is frozen out, and the NDP is fading; in 2000 it was the only region where, because of Alliance weakness, the Tories were still competitive

In 1993, the Liberals took well over 50% of the vote in every Atlantic province, and 31 of the 32 seats. The only survivor of the Liberal tide was Tory Elsie Wayne in Saint John. The Conservatives came second in the popular vote at 26.2%, with the NDP trailing at 5.4%. Reform made a respectable first impression in Nova Scotia (13.3%) and New Brunswick (8.5%), but not elsewhere. By 1997, the Liberals had become thoroughly unpopular in the region, while the NDP had chosen Nova Scotian Alexa McDonough as their new leader. The upshot of this was an unprecedented eight Atlantic seats for the NDP and 23.7% of the popular vote, a strong comeback to 13 seats for the Tories with 33.8% of the vote, and a two-thirds drop in Liberal seats to only 11 with 32.8% of the vote. Reform reversed its position to 13.1% of the vote in New Brunswick, and 9.7% in Nova Scotia, but still won no seats. In 2000, the Liberals bounced back to take 19 Atlantic seats with 40.7% of the vote, the Tories dropped to nine seats with 31.3%, and the NDP to four seats and 16.6% of the vote. The Canadian Alliance, although again winning no seats, improved its vote to 15.7% in New Brunswick while fading slightly to 9.6% in Nova Scotia — the only province in which the Alliance did worse in 2000 than Reform had done in 1997.

BOTH THE TORIES AND REFORM/ALLIANCE MUST ACCEPT THAT THEY ARE NOW REGIONAL PARTIES, EACH UNABLE TO BREAK OUT OF ITS REGIONAL BASE

In the context of the Tory-Alliance rivalry, the Tories' Atlantic "base" of nine seats and barely 30% of the vote cannot remotely compare with the Alliance base of 60 seats and over 50% of the vote in the three western provinces. After the Tory successes in the Atlantic in 1997, there were predictions that the region would be the springboard for a spectacular Tory comeback. But today, the Atlantic region is not really a Tory base at all — it is a Liberal base where the Tories are a distant second. The Alliance has also been marginally stronger in the Atlantic than the Tories have been in the West. And while the Alliance vote has been slowly growing in the Atlantic region, the Tory vote has been declining in the West. Without some accommodation with the Alliance, the best the Tories can hope for is to hold on to their existing Atlantic seats, and pray that the Alliance vote doesn't start cutting further into theirs, giving the Liberal party even more victories. Some comeback! Some base!

But at the same time, three elections after the disintegration of the Mulroney Conservatives, the Alliance remains, like Reform, essentially restricted to the four western provinces. Because of the refusal of the Conservative party either to disappear or to cooperate, the Alliance has been tantalizingly unable to win more than two seats in Ontario, and in the Atlantic region has succeeded only in coming close in one or two more.

The supporters and particularly the leadership of both parties must now finally accept that given the overwhelming superiority of the Liberals in Ontario, their gradual absorption of former NDP voters throughout the country, and even more significantly their gradual reconquest of their traditional base in Quebec, the only conceivable salvation for the two conservative parties is to combine forces once again, eventually within a single national party. The distribution of Canada's population, while changing ever so slowly in favour of Alberta and British Columbia, still means that for better or for worse, the 91 Commons seats west of Ontario and the 32 east of Quebec — 123 seats in all — cannot match Ontario's 103 seats plus Quebec's 75. The two central provinces control 178 seats in our 301-seat House, and the Liberals control most of the two central provinces. Even if Joe Clark were miraculously to win 66 seats in the next election, and reduce the Alliance to 12, nothing would have changed.

It is well known that political leaders have an infinite capacity for self-delusion — indeed it is probably a job requirement. But for the leader of a party that faces the realities which the Tories face today across the country, to continue to reject formal discussions about possible cooperation with the Alliance is either political blindness or personal egotism of truly breathtaking proportions. One can only marvel — and despair — at such intransigent and selfish disregard for the national interest. And one can only pray that the governing councils of the Progressive Conservative party may come to a clearer view of their duty to their country, before the Liberals have completely reasserted their traditional hold on Quebec and rendered the whole question moot.

As we saw in Chapter 4, it is not in the narrow personal interest of a party leader to lead himself potentially out of his job by combining with another party. Even Preston Manning, perhaps the most principled of recent party leaders, was somewhat taken aback when this happened to him. Perhaps the ordinary Canadians who regularly implore Messrs Clark and Day to resolve their differences and bring their two parties together are simply expecting too much of them. Be that as it may, in view of the depressing inability of all our current leaders to consider wider issues than their own status, they leave us with no choice but to turn to others to do the job that must be done. Unless both of them can demonstrate that they are prepared to lead the process sincerely and in good faith, Joe Clark and Stockwell Day should stand aside from the reunification process of their two parties on the grounds of a clear conflict of interest.

As an old saying has it, "If you want to lead, lead. If you want to follow, follow. But if you aren't going to do either, get the hell out of the way."

CHAPTER SEVEN

How to Resolve
the PC-Alliance Rivalry

How to Begin to Recreate a Second National
Party and Restore a Functioning Democracy
to Canada by the end of 2002

There are three essential premises on which any cooperation or unification discussions must be based. The first is that the two parties consider and treat each other as equals, and accept that neither one is simply going to fold itself into the other or disappear entirely: the only practical way for the two parties to eventually come together is to jointly form a new conservative party. The second is that in any unification talks, all the attributes and characteristics of any new party be open for discussion. And the third is that participants accept that each existing party is much more than its leader and its parliamentary caucus, and in fact consists of every paid-up member of the party, with each member having an equal voice in such major issues as these. The entire party membership must accordingly be consulted about the process and must ratify the outcome.

THE PROCESS MUST BE MEMBER-DRIVEN, NOT LEADER-DRIVEN

It follows from the last premise that the process must be driven primarily not by the party leaders or caucuses, but by the party members and their representatives. The members of both parties have elected national governing bodies to represent the membership in the day-to-day governance and management of party affairs. The Conservatives have both a national council and a management committee, while the Alliance has only a national council. These bodies, as the constitutionally delegated representatives of the party members, must initiate and carry forward the cooperation or unification process. And these bodies have a duty and responsibility to the people of Canada to put the national interest ahead of personal or partisan interests.

The first step is for the governing body of each party to give a formal mandate to one or more delegates — let's call them "conferees" — to make contact with the other party to open discussions. As previously mentioned, the Canadian Alliance National Council took this step in May 2001, instructing its then co-presidents, Ken Kalopsis of Ontario and Clayton Manness of Manitoba, to make an official approach to the Progressive Conservative party. In June, the council formed a Unity Committee consisting of six officers from the council and six from the Canadian Alliance caucus, with a similar mandate. Ideally, these conferees should not include either party's leader, in view of the strong perception that both men have a conflict of interest.

FIVE KEY SETS OF ISSUES, AND TWO STRATEGIC OPTIONS: EARLY UNIFICATION, OR FIRST AN ELECTORAL ALLIANCE

Once it has been established that each party is prepared at least to talk to the other "without prejudice", as the legal phrase goes, the next logical step is for the conferees to agree on an agenda and an urgent timetable for future discussions. There are five obvious topics that must be explored together by the conferees of each party, with a view to identifying first, areas of agreement, and second, any significant differences between the two parties:

1) policy issues, including possible ideological or cultural differences;
2) party governance issues;
3) name issues;
4) finance issues;
5) leader's election process issues.

A quick review of these five sets of issues should lead logically to one of three possible conclusions: (a) that the two parties should start by trying to negotiate an electoral pact, with each party retaining its independent existence; (b) that instead, the two parties should begin forthwith to discuss how they might actually recombine into a single conservative party; or (c) that there is no basis for any formal relationship whatsoever — the two parties are just too incompatible.

As most observers have pointed out, there can be no prospect of successful unification discussions unless both parties can first agree on the fundamental policy orientation that a unified party should adopt. We will return to this point later in this chapter. Assuming that basic policy questions can be agreed upon, the remaining four points should not present any major obstacles to an eventual agreement. Party governance issues are mostly technical, such as the frequency of meetings, the composition and method of choosing members of the governing body, the status of the youth wing, and so on. The most contentious issue may well turn out to be the name of the combined party, which should certainly include the word "Conservative" — on that much, at least, there should be no dispute.

If, on the other hand, the conferees decide that it is premature to consider unification, and conclude instead that an electoral pact is the best first step, then these five sets of issues will not have to be addressed. Each party would, for the present at least, retain its existing policies, governance, name, finances, and leadership. The following discussion of these five points assumes that the strategic option adopted is some form of unification of the two parties.

RETIRING EXISTING PARTY DEBT AND RESTRICTING FUTURE DEBT

Now that the Tories have liquidated the holdings of their Bracken House Trust (derived from the sale of an Ottawa building some years ago) and used the proceeds of some $4.5 million to pay down their loan at the CIBC to between $6 million and $9 million, the debt issue has become more manageable than ever. The Canadian Alliance finished the 2000 election owing some $2.3 million in election financing to its consortium of six banks. Given the ardent desire of Canada's financial community to see a single united national conservative party, raising funds to eliminate the combined debt of the two existing parties would not be difficult. It will also be important for the conferees to be aware of all conservatives' desire to operate their party in future on a debt-free basis as far as possible; they should thus recommend strict guidelines for keeping election spending, in particular, within the realistic fundraising limits of the party.

METHOD OF SELECTING THE LEADER (SEE ALSO BACKGROUNDER 4)

On the question of the best method for selecting a leader, both existing parties chose their current leader using the "one member, one vote" approach, favouring direct election by all the members over the delegated convention approach still followed by the Liberals. The main difference between the two conservative parties is that the Tory formula waters down — or evens out — possible regional inequalities in membership by giving 100 leadership votes to every riding, regardless of how many members it contains, to be distributed among the leadership candidates on the basis of the proportional vote in each riding. The Alliance, on the other hand, used an unadulterated form of direct democracy in the only leadership contest it has ever held, which was won by Stockwell Day. Having observed both methods, informed opinion seems to be leaning toward the Tory approach as offering the best guarantee against possible hijacking of the process by well-organized special interest groups.

However, there is a contrary view that the modern practice of permitting anybody to buy a party membership for $10 at virtually the last minute, for the sole purpose of voting for a particular leadership candidate, is highly damaging to the long-term stability of the party, and also encourages "packing" the membership lists with "instant" members who have no commitment to the general principles and aims of the party and who cannot be relied upon for future assistance after the leadership election is over. In theory, thousands of Liberals could buy Alliance memberships, elect the worst possible leader, and sit back and laugh at the results.

This problem has been intelligently discussed in a recent column for the Halifax *Daily News* by long-time Liberal Brian Flemming of Halifax, entitled "Phoney democracy ruins CA". This column is reproduced below as **BACKGROUNDER 4**.

TIMETABLE FOR DISCUSSIONS

As to the timetable for inter-party discussions, the governing bodies of the Tories and the Alliance should not underestimate the time that will be required simply to identify the various areas of agreement and disagreement, and to come up with a list of issues that require resolution. And once the issues to be resolved have been identified, the time-consuming process of actually resolving them must still take place. This may well involve the appointment of a number of joint committees, which will require adequate time for consultation and deliberation. It should not be forgotten that most of the people that would be involved in this process are volunteers, and cannot devote their full time to it.

For a single united party to be in the field, organized, and competitive for the next federal election, it should be launched at least twelve months in advance. Although the next election would normally be held no earlier than four years from the last one, that is fall, 2004, we have seen that a Liberal prime minister can be ruthless in using the power of dissolution to his partisan advantage. It is quite possible that the next election, like the last one, might be only three and a fraction years subsequent — especially if the Liberals choose a new leader in the meantime, who can use the excuse of wanting a personal mandate from Canadians. It would therefore be prudent to assume an election in 2003, which means that the conservative unification process, including the selection of a leader, should be completed in 2002.

If this timetable is to be followed, time is already very short. A detailed unification proposal would have to be submitted to a general meeting of each of the two parties in the first half of 2002. As mentioned, the Canadian Alliance has already set the date for its general assembly, which will take place April 4-7, 2002, in Edmonton. If approved by both meetings, the proposal would presumably require ratification by the entire party membership before a leadership election could be held in the fall of

2002. If this timetable is not met, the entire process will be delayed by six months to a year, and could then not be completed until 2003. This would put the new party, possibly with an inexperienced leader, at the mercy of another early election call, as happened to the Canadian Alliance in 2000.

One final point on process before turning to policy issues. In attempting to resolve any contentious issues that may be identified, the conferees and those assisting them may well have to recommend the occasional compromise, which may not satisfy everyone on all sides of the debate. In their discussions, the conferees should follow the principle of trying to satisfy the largest possible number of members and supporters of both parties, and should try not to recommend solutions that risk driving away substantial numbers of people. They may well decide that the assistance of a professional mediator might be helpful in some instances. The goal should be to make the tent as large as possible so as to attract the largest possible number of principled, democratic conservatives.

POLICY ISSUES

While the policies of the Canadian Alliance and the Progressive Conservative party are similar in most respects, there are two interrelated areas that require clarification. The first is the open-ended nature of the Alliance proposal for citizen-initiated referenda, and the second is the perception that referenda might be used (or abused) to call into question established rights and freedoms in Canada.

One can only admire the goal of the Reform party and the Canadian Alliance to increase the role and participation of ordinary citizens in the business of government, and to make elected legislators and the executive more accountable to all Canadians. Extending opportunities for democratic expression is an objective all conservatives can strongly support. However, many conservatives believe that in advocating more direct democracy, one must in the same breath acknowledge that it must operate within clear limits. The fact that a proposal might be endorsed in a referendum does not ensure that it is fair and just. It is particularly necessary to acknowledge this in a large, diverse and pluralistic federation where the balanced rights of all have evolved over time, and in many cases have been democratically enshrined in the constitution. Civilized societies everywhere have long accepted the fundamental principles of due process and the rule of law, in order to prevent the tyranny of arbitrary measures. One danger, of course, especially in a country composed of many vulnerable minorities, is the "tyranny of the majority", that US president Thomas Jefferson warned of in his first inaugural address in 1801:

> "All, too, will bear in mind this sacred principle, that though the will of the majority is in all cases to prevail, that will to be rightful must be reasonable; that the minority possess their equal rights, which equal law must protect, and to violate would be oppression."

Although minorities are naturally wary of any infringement of their rights by an unthinking or possibly intolerant majority, in the 2000 election, the group that became most concerned was not a minority at all, but a majority — Canadian women who were persuaded that the referendum proposals of the Canadian Alliance might be used to ban abortions. The ease with which the opponents of the Alliance were able to foment this concern is a perfect illustration of the need for extreme care and circumspection in formulating any proposals for referenda or plebiscites in our society, and for such referenda to be subject to clear legal limits.

The more general concern was the possibility that a minority might try to use citizen-initiated referenda to impose its own views on the wider community, by reopening debate on well-established rights and freedoms. Although this sounds like a contradiction in terms — how could a minority democratically impose its views on a majority? — it is not inconceivable that a well-organized and highly motivated minority could win a referendum in the face of an apathetic majority. And even if it lost the referendum, a great deal of time and public money would have been expended in a futile and divisive attempt to reopen an issue that was generally thought to have been settled.

Most Canadians would not agree that issues of personal conscience and behaviour, about which there is no unanimity of opinion, should be settled by a majority vote in a referendum. Where people feel deeply that their personal rights and freedoms are at stake, the idea that any majority could impose its views upon them is widely seen as inappropriate and unacceptable.

In these as in all other areas of apparent divergence between the two parties, we would do well to follow the advice in Act II of the Gilbert and Sullivan operetta, *The Gondoliers,* which former British prime minister Harold Macmillan kept always on his desk: *Quiet, calm deliberation disentangles every knot.*

CHAPTER EIGHT

The Critical Importance of Leadership

Leadership in Uniting Conservatives, in Surviving Liberal Attacks, and in Appealing to All Regions of the Country

1) Only a strong leader with truly national appeal can keep a single conservative party united and defeat the Liberals

The success or failure of a modern political party is almost totally dependent upon its leader. It is the leader who incarnates the party in the minds of voters, who is its main media face and spokesperson, and who principally determines its image, for better or for worse. Historically, Canadian party leaders have most often wielded immense power, dominating both their caucus and their party. It was partly in reaction against the virtual dictatorship of the leaders of the old parties that Reform and the Canadian Alliance tried to democratize their party structure, and keep more real power in the hands of the members and the national council of the party.

In theory, changes to the constitution of the Progressive Conservative party made during the leadership of Jean Charest had the same purpose. But since the accession of Joe Clark as leader, the democratization of his party has become a dead letter, and Clark now dominates his 11 caucus members, his management committee, his national council, and his 13,500 party members as much as Brian Mulroney ever did his own much larger army. Clark has been careful to install personal loyalists in all key positions, and two party presidents who dared to defy him were quickly shown the door, finally allowing Clark to put his own safe man in the job.

Although Preston Manning was always firmly in control of the party he founded, the same cannot be said of his successor. Stockwell Day failed spectacularly at the primary duty of any party leader, which is to keep his party together and united. He also failed to understand the critical importance for a new party leader of building a strong personal office team, headed by a loyal, respected and tough-minded chief of staff. Finally, as bemused Canadians saw on an almost daily basis, he had no sense of political strategy or leadership, other than to push out anyone who disagreed with him. He was not, to use the French term, a *rassembleur* — a leader who can bring together a number of disparate groups, a healer. He was never able to get ahead of the game, but was always on the defensive and reacting to events — a reaction that was usually too little and too late.

In Canada, any party leader who aspires to form a government also has the particular challenge of being at least minimally acceptable to all regions of this complex country, and of ensuring that their party wins not only a majority, but also seats in every province.

In Laurier, King, and St. Laurent, the Liberals were successful in choosing leaders who appealed to Canadians in every region, as being competent without being despotic, as understanding regional and other interests without being captive to them, and — at a minimum — as being able to keep the country together and the economy functioning. The only other Canadian leaders who have won majority support in all parts of the country were Tories Macdonald, Diefenbaker, and Mulroney, although the last two lost significant regional support after a single great sweep.

Even Western Canadians, who have frequently felt left out of our national government, were generally onside for Laurier's victories, for King's after 1925, and for St. Laurent until Diefenbaker became Tory leader in 1956, despite the rise and fall of several western-based third parties. (See **BACKGROUNDER 1**.) The West also supported Macdonald, Diefenbaker and Mulroney. But St. Laurent was the last Liberal leader to win a majority of the seats in Western Canada, taking 43 out of 72 in 1949. Except for parts of British Columbia, westerners generally stayed loyal to Diefenbaker until his departure in 1967, and to his Tory successors until 1993, when they switched to Reform. Remarkably, since 1949, the Liberals have never even come close to a majority of western and territorial seats — their best showings were Trudeau's 28 out of 70 in 1968, and Chrétien's 29 out of 89 in 1993 (Chrétien currently holds 17 of 91 western seats; Trudeau dropped to only two in 1980.

It is sometimes argued by western commentators that no Western Canadian party leader can ever succeed in the rest of the country — that the deck is stacked against them, that their upright moral and political principles will never be accepted in the sinful and socialist East. It is true that of the six party leaders who have gained strong support in all regions, three were from Quebec, two from Ontario, and only one — John Diefenbaker — from the West, namely Saskatchewan. Clearly, it is an advantage for a leader to be from central Canada, containing as it does 178 of the 301 seats in the House of Commons. But Diefenbaker (and before him R.B. Bennett) showed that being from Ontario or Quebec was not essential for success across the country, and several other central Canadian leaders — Pearson, Trudeau and Chrétien are examples — showed that it was not sufficient either. The most western seats that Pearson ever won in four elections was 10, while the fewest was one, in 1958.

While Diefenbaker's national sweep of 208 seats is proof that a western conservative *can* win, even in central Canada, there are two critical new elements in the electoral equation today that Dief did not have to face in 1958. The first is the presence of the Bloc Québécois in Quebec, and the second is the split between the Tories and the Canadian Alliance everywhere else.

Quebec: the presence of the Bloc Québécois ensures there will always be a "native son" party leader

Canadian history amply demonstrates several things about the federal voting patterns of francophone Quebecers. The first is that Quebecers tend to view provincial politics as the main event, and federal elections as something of a sideshow which they need not take as seriously. They have no problem supporting a third made-in-Quebec party with no chance to form a government, if they like the cut of its leader, or simply want to give the finger to the rest of the country. In this respect, they are not much different from Western Canadians. The second is that Quebecers often like to counterbalance the government they elect in Quebec City by supporting a different party in Ottawa.

But by far the major voting determinant for most Quebec francophones is that given the chance to vote for a native-son leader who is also a Quebec francophone, they will do so massively in preference to non-Quebec anglophone leaders, almost regardless of party affiliation. Diefenbaker's sweep of 50 of Quebec's 75 seats in 1958 was only possible because that election was one of the few in recent times in which *no* party had a Quebec francophone leader — it was a choice between Diefenbaker from

Saskatchewan or Pearson from Ontario. By the following election in 1962, a new francophone leader *had* appeared in the person of Réal Caouette, with his ragtag group of *Créditistes*. Caouette came virtually from nowhere to take 26 of Diefenbaker's seats in the province, reducing the Tories to 14 while Pearson took 35.

Once Pearson was succeeded by another Quebec francophone in the person of Pierre Trudeau, Quebecers resumed their practice of giving the Liberals the vast majority of their seats. The Liberals lost this Quebec advantage when they chose as their next leader John Turner, an ex-Quebecer whose French and political skills were both somewhat rusty. Turner had the misfortune to find himself up against a real Quebecer who was fully bilingual, Brian Mulroney, who confirmed the native-son rule by taking 58 Quebec seats in 1984 and 63 in 1988. But after Mulroney's departure, the Tories under Kim Campbell lost all but one of these seats, mainly to Lucien Bouchard's new Bloc Québécois, which took 54 seats in 1993.

What the Bloc Québécois has now done is to ensure that in every federal election, there will *always* be at least one Quebec francophone party leader, so that any anglophone leader who cannot communicate well in French will be at a fatal disadvantage. No Diefenbakers need apply. Even Jean Chrétien, a native Quebec francophone Liberal prime minister with every advantage, has never been able to win a majority of Quebec's seats against the Bloc in three tries. Chrétien managed only 19 Quebec seats in 1993, 26 in 1997, and 36 in 2000. The lesson for all parties is crystal clear: only a leader who is fluent in French, and who can demonstrate understanding and sympathy for the concerns of Quebecers, will have a hope of winning any substantial number of seats in Quebec.

Since none of the present leaders of the Tories, the Alliance, or the NDP is either a Quebecer or fully bilingual, none of these parties now has a realistic chance of winning seats in Quebec. While there may be the occasional exception such as lone current Tory incumbent André Bachand, the real battle in Quebec is solely between the Liberals and the Bloc, and the Liberals are gradually winning. Only if the next Liberal leader is not fully bilingual, and if another party chooses a leader who is, will that leader have a serious opportunity to make gains in Quebec. But because of the presence of the Bloc Québécois, for any party without a fully bilingual leader, Quebec will remain an electoral desert.

Outside Quebec: without Tory/Alliance cooperation, the Liberals will win forever

The second new factor that makes a Diefenbaker-or Mulroney-like sweep impossible today is the ongoing split between the Tories and the Canadian Alliance, originally created by the success of the Reform party in the three western provinces in 1993. It is the Tory/Alliance split outside Quebec that has handed Jean Chrétien three consecutive majorities — in a very real sense, Jean Chrétien owes his prime ministership to Preston Manning, and his 2000 majority to Joe Clark. Even worse, this split *guarantees* permanent Liberal governments until it is healed. This healing can be accomplished only by the collective leadership of the two parties, and the fact that it has not seriously begun to happen, even after eight years and three elections, is directly attributable to the undeniable — and irresponsible — failure of this leadership.

If any of these leaders still does not understand the inevitability of Liberal victories until they finally agree to cooperate, they need only look again at the results of the last election in November, 2000, together with current polls. In the Atlantic, the Liberals won 19 of 32 seats, and would win even more today. In Quebec, the Liberals won 36 of 75 seats, and would win even more today. In Ontario, the Liberals won 100 of 103 seats, and would win even more today. Only in the West, where the Liberals won just 17 of 91 seats, would they fail to win a majority of the seats today, although their western total would undoubtedly increase.

The leaders' failure to unite the divided opposition is keeping the Liberals in power with a minority of the vote

But the current electoral strength of the Liberals is actually a political illusion, an apparent fortress that is really built on sand. Only 40.8% of Canadians' votes were for Liberal candidates in 2000, which means that almost 60% of those who actually voted did not vote Liberal. In 1997 this figure was 61.5%, and in 1993 it was 58.7%. The problem is that instead of all voting for a single opposition party, in each election, voters split their non-Liberal votes among four different parties, three of which are largely confined to a single region. In 2000, for example, 25.5% of Canadian voters, mostly in the West, voted for the Alliance; 12.2%, mostly in the East, voted for the Tories; 10.7%, all in Quebec, voted for the Bloc; and 8.5% voted NDP. And since the national turnout in 2000 was only 61.2% of eligible voters, a record low, this means that almost two out of every five eligible Canadians did not bother to vote at all — many, no doubt, out of disillusionment with the divided opposition.

We saw in the previous section what Canadian conservatives must do in Quebec to attract current Bloc Québécois and Liberal voters: to begin with, they must have a bilingual leader. Outside Quebec, as long as the leaders of the Alliance and the Tories irresponsibly keep their parties divided, sub-divided and refusing even to talk officially to one another, they will fail to attract current Liberal voters, and current non-voters — not to mention current NDP voters. But with new leadership, and with full cooperation between the Tories and the Alliance, they could win the next election.

The Tories cannot displace the Alliance in the West, the Alliance cannot displace the Tories in the East

There are senior Tories who believe that the Canadian Alliance will totally collapse before the next election, and that simply by doing nothing, Joe Clark will be able to pick up the 64 western seats that the Alliance currently holds. There are two fatal flaws in this belief. The first is that the Alliance, despite its internal splits and leadership problems, will never totally collapse in Western Canada as long as surrendering to Joe Clark's Tories is the only alternative. A huge number of western Alliance supporters would, almost literally, rather die than admit defeat at the hands of Joe Clark, and they will support their western movement to the last ditch and the last man. Just look at the levels of support the Alliance enjoyed in the West in the 2000 election: 49.4% in British Columbia, 58.9% in Alberta, and 47.7% in Saskatchewan, which gave the Alliance 60 of the 74 seats in those three provinces.

The second flaw in the assumption of some PCs is the reality that even if the Alliance did largely collapse, most of its western supporters would not vote for the Clark Tories. Again, just look at the level of western support for Joe Clark in 2000: 7.3% in B.C., 13.5% in Alberta, and 4.8% in Saskatchewan — in each province, at least 42 points behind the Alliance. The only seat that Joe Clark won in these three provinces was his own, and recent polls clearly show that many of those western voters who may currently be fed up with the Alliance leadership debacle would vote for the Liberals before they would ever vote for Clark. Failing some accommodation between the two parties, it would take many elections and many years before the Tories could ever win anything close to the number of western seats the Alliance holds today. Again, it is squarely up to the leadership of both parties to stop fighting each other and work out the necessary accommodation.

Unfortunately, there is an equally implausible myth that is dear to the hearts of many western Alliance supporters, and that is that a western-based protest party founded on populism and social conservatism might still somehow succeed in Eastern Canada. This faction would like the Alliance to return to Reform's original ideological roots, consolidate its western base, and become in effect the Bloc Québécois of the West. No doubt this would be a successful electoral strategy in the three western provinces, but it would virtually rule out any success east of Manitoba.

But if this strategy was part of a larger national strategy of dividing up the country between the Alliance and the Tories under an electoral pact, it would have the merit of guaranteeing the survival and even the prospering of the Tories in the Atlantic region, where in addition to their nine federal seats they also hold three provincial governments — and may soon hold four. The Atlantic Tories would have no serious rivals on the right, and they would continue unchallenged in their historic role in the Atlantic region as the main alternative to the Liberal party.

In Ontario, because of our leaders' intransigence, divided we lose, and lose, and lose...

What of Ontario, the new Liberal bastion since 1993, and the astonishing foundation of three consecutive Liberal majorities? Since 1993, Ontario has been a wasteland for both Tories and Reform/Alliance. Over the three elections, the Tory vote share in Ontario has been 17.6% under Kim Campbell, 18.8% under Jean Charest, and only 14.4% under Joe Clark. Meanwhile, in 1993 and 1997, Reform under Preston

Manning got 20.1% and 19.1%, while the Canadian Alliance under Stockwell Day took 23.6% in 2000. In the first two elections, both Campbell and Charest were handicapped in Ontario by the Mulroney connection, while Manning could not overcome his image as an oddball western fundamentalist. In 2000, Stockwell Day pulled clearly ahead of Joe Clark in Ontario, but to little avail in terms of seats. It is highly revealing that the combined Ontario vote total of both parties has stayed much the same throughout the three elections, at 37.7%, 37.9%, and 38%. Obviously, both parties are fishing in the same restricted, largely rural Ontario pond, busily trying to take the same votes from one another, but completely failing to expand their voter pool.

There are several reasons for this failure, but in the end they all come down once again to inadequate, unimaginative and overly partisan leadership. It is not only that none of the leaders of the two conservative parties has been able to attract even a quarter of Ontario's voters, but even more importantly, their very inability to work together as practical politicians continues to repel the vast majority of mainstream Ontarians. The Alliance's image of narrowness, incompetence, and unprofessionalism, and the Clark Tories' image of irrelevance, hubris, and obsession with old quarrels, have destroyed the credibility of both parties in the eyes of most Ontario voters. As mentioned already, this reaction is summed up in the refrain heard everywhere today, and not just in Ontario: *Why can't you people get your act together?*

Because of this failure of leadership, in Ontario we have witnessed a stand-off after a deadlock followed by a stalemate between the Alliance and the Tories, who most recently succeeded brilliantly in giving 100 Ontario seats to the Liberals (with 51.5% of the votes, but with the support of only 29.7% of the registered voters, many of whom simply stayed home), two seats to the Alliance, and zero to the Tories.

...but united, we could win: it is entirely up to the Alliance and Tory party leadership

In Ontario at least, this is truly a situation where the whole would be much greater than the sum of the parts. A united conservative party under the right leader could easily recapture the traditional level of Ontario support, and of seats, that conservatives could generally count on before 1993. If such a united party could also hold the seats the Alliance holds in the West, and the seats the Tories hold in the East — and there is no reason why it could not — it would immediately become competitive with the Liberals. Alternatively, an electoral pact under which the two parties agreed not to run against one another in any riding might accomplish the same objective.

While the need for the Tories and Reform to come together was apparent to many as early as 1993, it was not politically conceivable until after the election of 1997. The results of that election finally convinced Preston Manning that his Reform party could never break out of the West as long as the Tories survived in Central and Eastern Canada. Not long afterwards, both Jean Charest and his party concluded, after coming a dismal fifth once again, with only 20 seats, that as leader he would be wise to seek greener pastures in Quebec. Although Manning was willing to talk, Charest made it clear before his departure that he was not — like his mentor, Brian Mulroney, he could never forgive Manning for destroying the western base of the PC party, and for authorizing television spots in the 1997 campaign that appeared anti-Quebec.

After having floated the idea for some time, Preston Manning formally launched his United Alternative campaign at the end of May, 1998. Charest had already rejected the idea in a fighting speech to his party's governing body on February 28, 1998 in Ottawa, in the following terms:

"Preston Manning speaks of a united alternative. They have no plan for keeping our country together, but they propose a plan to make our parties come together. Well, hell hasn't frozen over yet. This can never happen, if only for one reason: for every proposal Preston Manning has to make Canada worse, we have ten to make it work. Make no mistake: a united alternative means taking over 130 years of tradition and throwing it away. Frankly, the only alternative worth considering is the Progressive Conservative alternative. Reform pits one region against another. I prefer to compare one country against another. Preston Manning likes to talk about Canada's regions. I like to talk about Canada."

However, Charest announced his resignation as Tory leader just over a month later, on April 3, 1998, and for seven or eight months, until Joe Clark was elected leader of the Tories on November 14, 1998, there was a window of opportunity during which the two parties might have begun discussions. But as interim Tory leader, Elsie Wayne did not believe she had a mandate to do so, nor did she seek one. Of the four Tory leadership candidates other than Clark, only Michael Fortier was openly in favour of talking to Reform, and he even promised to attend the United Alternative conference. Brian Pallister privately claimed to favour discussions with Reform, but refused to say so publicly. Hugh Segal was emotionally opposed to dealing with Manning, but understood the imperatives of the electoral arithmetic, and as leader, would probably have been pragmatic about it. David Orchard saw Manning as the devil incarnate.

Joe Clark has been absolutely consistent. In another of the classic misjudgments that have marked his career, from the moment he began musing about running to succeed Jean

Charest, he has refused to have anything to do with Reform, Preston Manning, the United Alternative, the Canadian Alliance, or Stockwell Day. They will self-destruct, the party is just a flash in the pan, it is only a matter of time, they will all come home to the grand old Progressive Conservative Party of Canada, and a grateful country will turn again to me — this has been his constant theme.

All of these leaders on both sides have failed Canadians, and in blindly refusing to acknowledge reality, they have also failed the members of their own parties. Without dealing with the other party, no PC or Alliance leader can ever lead his troops to a national victory, and to pretend otherwise is profoundly dishonest. What is needed now is some evidence of true national leadership — leadership that is prepared to look beyond narrow personal and partisan interests and animosities, and that will instead consider the vital interests of Canadians as a whole, and the long-term welfare of our country. Unfortunately, such leadership appears to be in extremely short supply among conservatives in Canada today.

2) Note to future leaders: how to survive Liberal character assassination attempts

We saw in Chapter 1 (and will see in more detail in BACK-GROUNDER 3C below) how the federal Liberal party has so successfully adopted the American political practice and techniques of negatively "defining" the image of their adversaries, so as to make them appear to the average voter as dangerous, scary, and unfit to run the country. A recent American book, *The Art of Political War and Other Radical Pursuits* by David Horowitz, explains in detail the six principles of modern political warfare, and how to deal with enemy assaults. The following excerpt is quoted with permission, slightly adapted to fit the Canadian context — mainly by replacing "Republican", "Democrat", and so on with bracketed Canadian names and references. Comments by the authors are in italics.

*   *   *   *   *

"The (Canadian Alliance) claims to be the party of personal responsibility, yet it has become a party that takes no responsibility for the predicaments in which it finds itself. Instead (conservatives) blame bias in the media, or the liar in (24 Sussex Drive), or their unprincipled opponents, or even the immorality of the (Canadian) people to explain their defeats.

"When (conservatives) complain about forces they cannot control, they behave like victims and give up the power to determine their fate. (Liberals) will be (Liberals). They will be unprincipled and lie. If (conservatives) go into battle expecting (Liberals) to be better than they are, they will only set themselves up for political ambush. Instead of complaining, (conservatives) should be asking themselves: How do the (Liberals) do it? How do they get away with it? What do they know that makes them able to package a bankrupt political agenda and sell it successfully to the (Canadian) voter?

"There are six principles of political war that the left understands, but conservatives do not:

1. Politics is war conducted by other means

In political warfare you do not fight just to prevail in an argument, but to destroy the enemy's fighting ability. (Conservatives) often seem to regard political combats as they would a debate before the Oxford Political Union, as though winning depended on rational arguments and carefully articulated principles. But the audience of politics is not made up of Oxford dons, and the rules are entirely different.

You have thirty seconds to make your point. Even if you had time to develop an argument, the audience you need to reach (the undecided and those in the middle who are not paying much attention) would not get it. Your words would go over some of their heads and the rest would not even hear them (or quickly forget) amidst the bustle and pressure of daily life. Worse, while you have been making your argument, the other side has already painted you as a mean-spirited borderline racist controlled by religious zealots, securely in the pockets of the rich. Nobody who sees you this way is going to listen to you in any case. You are politically dead.

Politics is war. Don't forget it.

2. Politics is a war of position

In war there are two sides: friends and enemies. Your task is to define yourself as the friend of as large a constituency as possible compatible with your principles, while defining your opponent as the enemy whenever you can. The act of defining combatants is analogous to the military concept of choosing the terrain of battle. Choose the terrain that makes the fight as easy for you as possible. But be careful. ...Politics takes place in a pluralistic framework, where constituencies are diverse and often in conflict. 'Fairness' and 'tolerance' are the formal rules of democratic engagement. If you appear mean-spirited or too judgmental, your opponent will more easily define you as a threat, and therefore as the enemy (see principle 4).

3. In political warfare, the aggressor usually prevails

(Conservative parties) often pursue a conservative strategy of waiting for the other side to attack. In football, this is known as a 'prevent defence.' In politics it is the strategy of losers.

Aggression is advantageous because politics is a war of

position, which is defined by images that stick. By striking first, you can define the issues as well as your adversary. Defining the opposition is the decisive move in all political war. Other things being equal, whoever is on the defensive generally loses.

In attacking your opponent, take care to do it effectively. 'Going negative' increases the risk of being defined as an enemy. Therefore, it can be counterproductive. Ruling out the negative, however, can incur an even greater risk. (…) Never say 'never' in political battles. It is an art, not a science.

4. Position is defined by fear and hope

The twin emotions of politics are fear and hope. Those who provide people with hope become their friends; those who inspire fear become enemies. Of the two, hope is the better choice. By offering people hope and yourself as its provider, you show your better side and maximize your potential support.

But fear is a powerful and indispensable weapon. If your opponent defines you negatively enough, he will diminish your ability to offer hope. This is why (Liberals) are so determined to portray (conservatives) as mean-spirited and hostile to minorities, the middle class, and the poor. (…)

(Liberals) have successfully associated the Religious Right with moralistic intolerance. They have been helped by intolerant pronouncements from religious leaders and by political groups with toxic names like the 'Moral Majority' and the 'Christian Coalition.' As a result, it is easy for liberals to portray them as a threat to any constituency that does not share their values. 'They will impose their morals on you.' It does not matter whether this is true or not. Once a negative image has taken hold, the target is wounded — often mortally — in the political battle.

To combat this form of attack, it is important to work away from the negative image your opponent wants to pin on you. If you know you are going to be attacked as morally imperious, it is a good idea to lead with a position that is inclusive and tolerant. If you are going to be framed as mean-spirited and ungenerous, it is a good idea to put on a smile and lead with acts of generosity and charity. This will provide a shield from attack. When Clinton signed the welfare reform bill he made sure he was flanked by two welfare mothers.

Symbols are so powerful that if you manipulate them cleverly, as (liberals) do, you can even launch mean-spirited attacks on your opponents and pretend to be compassionate while doing it. (Liberals) understand, for example, that positioning themselves as victims gives them a licence to attack. A gay politician … can assault an opponent and call it self-defence. (*Authors' note: In the same way, Liberals can get away with using a Jewish woman such as Elinor Caplan to slander Alliance members as racists.*)

But remember this: using fear as a weapon can be dangerous. Enemies inspire fear; friends do not. That is why (Chrétien) lets his surrogates do the dirty work. When and how to use fear is a political art. If you are a white male in a culture whose symbols have been defined by liberals, be careful when you go on the offensive, and be sure to surround yourself with allies who are neither male nor white.

5. The weapons of politics are symbols evoking fear and hope

The most important symbol is the candidate (*Authors' note: especially the leader*). Does the candidate, in his own person, inspire fear or hope? Voters want to know: is the candidate someone who cares about people like me? Do I feel good about him, or does he put me on guard? Would I want to sit next to him at dinner? Style, especially for high public office, is as important as any issue or strategy. Jack Kennedy — a relatively inexperienced do-nothing congressman and senator — was able to win a national election merely by reciting problems and then repeating the litany 'we can do bettah.' Why? In part it was because he was handsome, witty, young and charming — and was not a zealot.

Republicans lose a lot of political battles because they come across as hard-edged, scolding, scowling, and sanctimonious. A good rule of thumb is to be just the opposite. You must convince people you care about them before they will care about what you have to say. When you speak, do not forget that a sound bite is all you have. Whatever you have to say, make sure to say it loud and clear. Keep it simple and keep it short — a slogan is always better. Repeat it often. Put it on television. Radio is good, but with few exceptions, only television reaches a public that is electorally significant. In politics, television is reality.

Of course, you have a base of supporters who will listen for hours to what you have to say if that is what you want. In the battles facing you, they will play an important role. Therefore, what you say to them is also important. But it is not going to decide elections. The audiences that will determine your fate are audiences that you will first have to persuade. You will have to find a way to reach them, get them to listen, and then to support you. With these audiences, you will never have time for real arguments or proper analyses. Images — symbols and sound bites — will always prevail. Therefore, it is absolutely essential to focus your message and repeat it over and over again. For a candidate, this means the strictest discipline. Lack of focus will derail your message. If you make too many points, your message will be diffused and nothing will get through. The result will be the same as if you had made no point at all.

The same is true for the party as a whole. (Liberals) have a party line. When they are fighting an issue they focus their agenda. Every time a (Liberal) steps in front of the cameras there is at least one line in his speech that is shared with his colleagues. 'Tax breaks for the wealthy at the expense of the poor' is one example. Repetition ensures that the message will get through. When (conservatives) speak, they all march to a different drummer. There are many messages instead of one. One message is a sound bite. Many messages are a confusing noise.

Symbols and sound bites determine the vote. These are what hit people in the gut before they have time to think. And these are what people remember. Symbols are the impressions that last, and therefore that ultimately define you. Carefully chosen words and phrases are more important than paragraphs, speeches, party platforms and manifestos. What you project through images is what you are.

The faces that represent (conservatives) are also images. In a pluralistic community, diversity is important. Currently, too many (conservative) faces (what you see on your television screen) are (Western Canadian) white men.

(Canada) is based on the idea that individual merit is what counts. As conservators of (this) principle, we reject artificial diversity and racial quotas. But this is political warfare. Images are what count. The image is the medium, and the medium is the message. Therefore, diversity is more than important. It is crucial to becoming a national majority. But it is also crucial because it is just. As conservatives, as defenders of (the) democratic principle, we want every constituency to feel included.

6. Victory lies on the side of the people

This is the bottom line for each of the principles and for all of the principles. You must define yourself in ways that people understand. You must give people hope in your victory, and make them fear the victory of your opponent. You can accomplish both by identifying yourself and your issues with the underdog and the victim, with minorities and the disadvantaged, with the ordinary Janes and Joes.

It is what (Liberals) do best, and (conservatives) often neglect to do at all. Every political statement by a (Liberal) is an effort to say: '(Liberals) care about women, children, minorities, working (Canadians), and the poor; (conservatives) are mean-spirited, serve the rich, and don't care about you.' This is the (Liberals') strategy of political war. If (conservatives) are to win the political war and become a national majority they have to turn these images around.

They also have to make their campaigns a cause. (…)

In a democracy, the cause that fires up passions is the cause of the people. That is why politicians like to run 'against Washington' (*or Ottawa*) and against anything that represents the 'powers that be.' As the left has shown, the idea of justice is a powerful motivator. It will energize the troops and fuel the campaigns that are necessary to win the political war.

(Conservatives) believe in economic opportunity and individual freedom. The core of their ideas is justice for all. If they could make this intelligible to the (Canadian) electorate, they would make themselves the party of the (Canadian) people."

*   *   *   *   *

What a pity that the Canadian Alliance campaign team had not grasped these principles before the last election. Seen in this context, the entire Stockwell Day campaign was an object lesson in how not to run one — from the original "agenda of respect" and refusing to strike the first blow, through actually helping the Liberal campaign to define him as a scary religious zealot, then being constantly on the defensive, allowing himself to be manipulated into inspiring fear rather than hope, not having a clear and focussed message or slogan, giving rambling speeches with no succinct sound bite, trying to symbolize the entire national campaign all by himself without making use of his many minority and women candidates, and so on.

To be fair to Stockwell Day, he was ruthlessly sandbagged by the Liberal high command when they called the election only weeks after his debut in the major leagues of national politics. No one doubts his good will or hard work; but in hindsight, he simply wasn't ready for prime time. Unfortunately, he and his closest advisers appear to have learned little from the experience.

But the rest of us must learn vicariously, and the lesson we must never forget is that the Liberals will do everything in their power to destroy the image and credibility of any potential conservative leader who dares so much as to stick his or her head above the parapet. They will begin their attacks, not directly but through their surrogates in the media and elsewhere, before the target even realizes what is happening. The Jean Chrétien Liberal team have become masters at the black art of negatively branding their opponents before the game has even begun, ensuring (in David Horowitz's graphic phrase) that they are "politically dead" even before they step onto the ice.

This is not to say that the other side is virginal or blameless. A neutral American professional would probably say that they are simply far less competent than the Liberals. They have not fully mastered how to be effective without being excessive, thereby giving their opponent the opportunity to strike the pose of a wronged and wounded victim. A perfect example of this amateurism was the Tory television ad in 1993 that drew attention to Jean Chrétien's facial paralysis. Within hours of its appearance, the Liberal campaign successfully claimed that this was truly dirty pool, and the embarrassed Tories were forced to withdraw the spot. In doing the essential job of "making the other guy the issue", make sure that your efforts don't backfire on your own campaign.

But the stakes are too high, and the future of our country is too important, for us to simply throw in the towel. Conservatives must learn to anticipate Liberal smears and to defend ourselves effectively against them. In short, we must become as politically professional and expert as our opponents, while remaining true to our principles in a way that they do not.

And we must remember that the Liberal party is not a truly national party. It has been unable to win majority support in Western Canada for over half a century, and is still as far from that goal as ever. In the past fifty years, only the conservative parties of John Diefenbaker and Brian Mulroney have succeeded in uniting all parts of Canada behind them at the same time. Although it has not happened often, it is a salutary and productive experience to have most Canadians in all parts of the country on the same side, instead of the standard Liberal operating procedure of pitting region against region. It is time that it happened again.

◇ **CHAPTER NINE**

Conclusion

How do we get there from here? How do we bring the Canadian Alliance and the Progressive Conservatives into harness together in time for the next election, under new leadership that can appeal to all Canadians?

There are five prerequisites to taking the first steps toward cooperation or reunification in 2002. First, formal talks between the Canadian Alliance and the Tories must be well advanced by the time a new Alliance leader is chosen in March, 2002. Second, all legitimate obstacles to these formal discussions must be dealt with urgently so that talks can proceed productively. Third, a discussion paper about possible approaches to cooperation between the two parties should be widely circulated and discussed. Fourth, the elements of both parties (and the general public) that understand the need for cooperation in order to defeat the Liberals must make their views known to the respective party leaderships privately and publicly, forcefully and effectively. And fifth, a serious search process for new national leadership of conservative forces in Canada must be undertaken.

TORY-ALLIANCE NEGOTIATIONS MUST BE WELL UNDER WAY BEFORE A NEW ALLIANCE LEADER IS CHOSEN

There is much media speculation about who should be the next leader of the Canadian Alliance. Under current circumstances, the best leader for the Canadian Alliance is no leader, or rather an interim leader who can allow the governing bodies of the Alliance and the Tories to get on quickly with formal discussions about electoral cooperation. For the Alliance, rushing into a leadership election would have the same effect as did the Tory leadership race after the resignation of Jean Charest — the window of opportunity for serious discussions with the Tories will quickly close, as attention turns inward and factions line up behind their respective favourites. If this opportunity is missed, it may not come again for several years, as the next leader of the Alliance is likely to believe (wrongly) that he can do much better than Manning or Day, without the need for any accommodation with the Tories. This was the case with Joe Clark when he succeeded Jean Charest. It would be tragic if this "Joe Clark syndrome" infected the Alliance before serious talks with the PCs — whether aimed at an electoral pact or at unification — were solidly on track.

The only way this might be avoided is for all candidates to pledge that as leader, their first act would be to seek an accommodation with the Progressive Conservatives. But such discipline is highly improbable, as it is counter-intuitive to expect most leadership candidates to campaign on leading their troops into an alliance with what was so recently the enemy camp. A leadership campaign, by its nature, will only bring out more calls for a return to the founding principles of Reform, and for new vigour and commitment in the fight to win, in Preston Manning's phrase, "150 seats plus one", while ignoring every other party.

LEGITIMATE OBSTACLES TO NEGOTIATIONS MUST BE DEALT WITH FIRST

Many members of the Canadian Alliance are convinced that there is no conceivable constellation of concessions or compromises that will ever bring Joe Clark to the negotiating table in good faith — not even a stark offer for all of them to meekly join the Progressive Conservative party as it now exists. Their scepticism is understandable, given Clark's past performance, and his illegitimate insistence that he would never negotiate as long as the hapless Stockwell Day was in the picture, even though Day was the duly elected leader. How would Clark react to a similar demand from the Alliance side about his own departure, which while politically wise, would be equally illegitimate as a condition for beginning any talks? Nevertheless, there are real signs that Clark and his high command are finally realizing the urgent need to talk to *someone*, even if it is only the dissident group of Alliance MPs. In any difficult negotiation where, initially, trust between the parties is virtually non-existent, it is often necessary to swallow one's pride simply to open communications, provided the ultimate goal is not compromised. In this spirit, both parties must work to remove any real obstacles to beginning serious talks, which in any case should be conducted mainly at the party-to-party level, not leader-to-leader.

If, as many suspect, Joe Clark has no serious intention of negotiating with the Alliance in good faith, it would be easy for him to invent excuses why he cannot enter talks "just now." To an interim or temporary leader succeeding Stockwell Day, he can say that this person has no mandate from the Alliance as a whole. If a new leader is chosen, he can easily find fault with something said or done during the leadership campaign. And since the results of his (unscientific) survey of his own membership's preferences have not been made public, Clark can continue to interpret them in whatever way suits his purpose. Finally, Clark seems able to dictate every move to his tame national council, which will not defy him even though a majority of its members may privately disagree with his course of action.

All by himself, Joe Clark can continue to keep the Liberals in power, as he has managed to do in both his incarnations as Tory leader.

NOW IS THE TIME FOR ALL GOOD TORIES TO COME TO THE AID OF THEIR *COUNTRY*

It is inconceivable that the great mass of Canadian conservatives should permit the stubbornness and shortsightedness of a handful of narrowly and misguidedly partisan politicos to forever frustrate achieving the goal of conservative unity, which alone can save the country from perpetual Liberal domination. Not only the so-called "silent majority" of conservatives, but also their recognized elders and key supporters from both parties, must come forward and bring their considerable influence to bear on the course of events.

It is not enough to privately bemoan the current state of affairs and simply throw up your hands, or pass the buck to someone else. Canadians in a position to help bring the parties together have a moral duty to stand up and be counted. We need the skills and prestige of former ministers such as Don Mazankowski, Bill McKnight, Jake Epp, Michael Wilson, Barbara McDougall, Gilles Loiselle, Elmer McKay and John Crosbie, and of their former leader, Brian Mulroney. We need the public counsel of former Tory premiers such as Peter Lougheed, Grant Devine, Gary Filmon and Bill Davis. The sizeable number of Tory senators who privately know the need for accommodation must speak out publicly. Finally, by refusing to make any public comment on the need for federal conservative unity, using the tiresome excuse that federal matters are of no concern to them, several of Canada's five Tory premiers are simply playing the Liberals' game. Despite the obvious tactical advantage of having the federal Liberals to blame for many of their provincial problems, can it really be true that Ralph Klein, Mike Harris, Bernard Lord, Pat Binns and John Hamm actually *want* their fellow Canadians to labour under a majority Liberal government in Ottawa forever? If not, they should light a public candle instead of just privately cursing the darkness.

And the founder of the Reform party, and godfather of the Canadian Alliance, Preston Manning, must also take a consistent and outspoken public stand in favour of cooperation between his former followers and the federal Tories, who must now finally come together to defeat their common enemy.

There is one particular category of party supporters who should also make their views known, publicly if possible but privately if they prefer, and that is the major financial contributors to each party. For eight years they have been spending millions of dollars to finance an inconclusive war between two conservative factions, while the real opponent escapes virtually unscathed. Those contributors who wish to see a united conservative effort against the Liberals should make it clear that while significant funding is available for this purpose, there will be no more money if it is merely to be wasted on further fratricidal and internecine battles.

A DISCUSSION PAPER SHOULD BE CIRCULATED, PROPOSING TO BEGIN WITH A GEOGRAPHICAL DIVISION OF SEATS

A helpful tool in attempting to determine the most effective way for the two parties to begin cooperating with one another would be a public discussion paper, in which one or two possible options are explored and analyzed in as neutral a fashion as possible. As a start, the two parties should probably consider a version of the simplest, least disruptive, and easiest form of cooperation: an electoral alliance. This would allow each party to retain its institutional integrity and independence, while still having the virtue of ending the ongoing war of attrition between them.

The most natural approach to an electoral alliance, given the respective regional strengths of the two parties, would be a simple geographic division of seats. A proposal for discussion might be that the Alliance would nominate candidates in all seats west of Ontario (91 seats), while the Tories would not, except for their two incumbent MPs who would be unopposed by Alliance candidates should they wish to run again. The Tories would run candidates in all seats east of Ontario (107 seats), while the Alliance would not; there are currently no Alliance incumbents in this region of the country. In Ontario (103 seats), the allocation of constituencies to each party would have to be determined by negotiation between the two parties, perhaps based loosely on past electoral performance or on some other regional or numerical criteria, but in the end, on which party's candidate would have the best chance of winning the seat. Again, the two incumbent Alliance MPs in Ontario would be unopposed by Tories, should they wish to run in the next election.

The geographic approach to an electoral alliance is much simpler than an attempt to arrange joint nominations, whereby every candidate would in effect be running for both parties at once. With joint candidacies, it would be necessary to decide which party name, which leader and which policies each candidate will run under, and how election fundraising and expenditures would be managed. With a territorial division, these questions do not arise. But the geographic approach does require an understanding, which is not easily enforceable, that the supporters of both parties will support the nominated candidate in every riding, even where that candidate is of the other party. Practically speaking, this is unlikely to be a problem except perhaps in Ontario, as the Alliance is generally quite weak in areas where the Tories are strong, and vice versa.

A territorial division of seats also requires an agreement as to who will be prime minister or opposition leader, depending on the election results, and on parliamentary cooperation between the two caucuses. If, after the election, the combined caucuses are large enough to form a government, presumably the leader of the largest caucus would be prime minister; but this must be made absolutely clear beforehand, as must the position to be given to the other leader.

Any electoral alliance would have to be ratified by the membership of each party. Ideally, it would also be seen as a temporary arrangement — an interim step on the way to a single party — to apply only for the next election unless renewed thereafter with the consent of both parties.

CAN ONLY LIBERALS FIGURE OUT HOW TO BECOME PRIME MINISTER? SOMEWHERE, THERE IS A CANADIAN CONSERVATIVE BOTH READY AND ABLE TO BECOME PRIME MINISTER IN 2004

The ship can be made ready to sail, but she will not reach safe harbour unless the right captain is in command. As we have all seen, this is not an easy position to fill. One difficulty is that many of those most eager to try are often the least qualified, while many of the most qualified are not eager to try.

It is not difficult to draw up a list of desirable qualifications for the next conservative prime minister of Canada. The person should be roughly from 35 to 60 years of age, fluently bilingual, experienced in federal politics, and a good communicator. The person should have demonstrated leadership qualities, good judgment, the ability to assemble and inspire a strong team, and a basic understanding of modern political strategy and campaign techniques. While a strong ego is obviously needed, it should be tempered by a measure of humility and the ability not to take oneself too seriously, and a high level of self-discipline. The person must have strong personal convictions, but be able to work closely with others who may not share all of them. The best modern example of a highly effective conservative leader of this type was Ronald Reagan, who recognized that someone who agrees with you 80 percent of the time is an 80 percent friend, not a 20 percent enemy.

There are in today's House of Commons 78 members of Parliament who would describe themselves as conservatives. There are many other former MPs, including many former federal ministers, in the same category. A number of them have all the qualities that are required. If the definition of federal political experience is expanded to include non-elected experience in Ottawa, the field of qualified people increases substantially. If this requirement is dropped entirely (at some risk), then the hundreds of people with provincial political experience in conservative governments and parties, including successful premiers and former premiers and many ministers, can also be added to the list.

The challenge facing all conservatives, and the many other Canadians who are deeply worried about the dangers of a one-party state, is to identify at least one properly qualified individual and then, by offering to assemble a team and resources to help him or her win the leadership, to persuade that person to make the considerable personal sacrifice required to serve our country in public life.

In the long run, however, it will not be enough merely to win the leadership of the Canadian Alliance or the federal PC party. Indeed, there is a risk that in gaining the leadership of one of these (today) essentially regional parties, a new leader might in the process come to be seen as less acceptable outside the region in question — as not yet qualified for truly national leadership. In the long run, a truly national leader must be the leader of a truly national party. Seen in this light, it is more understandable that the best candidates for leadership may not come forward until such a national party has been recreated. As in Canadian novelist W.P. Kinsella's book *Shoeless Joe* (on which the film *Field of Dreams* was based), we must therefore have faith that if we build it, they will come. But potential leaders should also recognize that we need their assistance in the difficult task of building the single national conservative party Canada must eventually have.

In any multi-party democracy — and especially in a country as large and diverse as Canada — a central function of a successful political party is to integrate and conciliate within a single organization the various regional and sectoral interests that are often in conflict with one another. This is not to say that a successful national party must be bereft of ideology, as some conservatives seem to conclude from their observation of the Liberals and the Mulroney Conservatives. But it does mean that in addition to standing for a coherent ideological position, a successful national conservative party must *also* exercise the classic "brokerage" function which is essential in keeping the party — and the country — together. As we have learned to our great cost since 1993, without brokerage politics, conservatives end up with broken politics. With a capable and qualified leader, a Canadian conservative party *can* be rebuilt that is both truly national and truly conservative — and is politically successful at the same time.

THE CHANCES OF SUCCESS, AND THE CONSEQUENCES OF FAILURE

In light of the open warfare between the two parties since 1993, and particularly considering the damage caused to both the Canadian Alliance and the Progressive Conservatives under the leadership of Stockwell Day and Joe Clark respectively, it is difficult to be optimistic about the likelihood of an effective alliance between the parties occurring in time to be fully successful in the next election. And yet, this would be so simple to accomplish, if only the political vision and will were present at the top of both parties.

Assuming that the remaining few thousand members of the Progressive Conservative party continue to allow a delusional Joe Clark, and his blindly obedient palace guard, to pursue their current strategy of pretending to want to negotiate while actually frustrating all efforts to find real accommodation between the two parties, the Alliance (and all Canadians) will have to accept reluctantly that there will be no deal with the Tories as long as Clark is their leader. The Alliance will then be faced with two broad options for its future, which will be reflected in its forthcoming leadership race.

If the Tories will not cooperate, either the Alliance must find a new leader with the desire and the ability to rebuild a truly national party that can appeal to a majority of Canadians despite Tory resistance, or it must accept the failure of Preston Manning's vision of a western-based party being able to break into Ontario and beyond in the face of this resistance. If the party pursues the first path, it will have to attempt once again in the next election to do what Stockwell Day so signally failed to do in 2000, namely to attract enough voters away from Clark and the Liberals to win a significant number of seats in Ontario and the Atlantic. Even if this strategy is successful, it will be difficult for the Alliance to win enough seats to form a government as long as Clark insists on running candidates against it in every seat. In the alternative, the Canadian Alliance must revert to the original mission of the Reform party of 1993 and before, and become once again the Bloc Québécois of the west. Up to a point, this is a perfectly defensible strategy, as under a strong new western leader the Alliance should easily be able to hold the 64 western seats it won in 2000, and perhaps gain even more. This at least has the merit of keeping seats out of Liberal hands, as the Bloc itself may continue to do in Quebec, and the Tories to a small degree in the Atlantic provinces. But this strategy leaves unanswered the great question of Ontario.

It is helpful at this point to go back to first principles. In a useful article in the *National Post* of June 15, 2001 — reprinted below as BACKGROUNDER 5 — University of Calgary political science professor Tom Flanagan (director of research for the Reform Party, 1991-92) describes five possible models for inter-party relations, ranging from unilateral action to outright merger. He points out that the strategy of unilateral action does not require the consent or cooperation of any other party.

If the Tories refuse even an electoral pact for Ontario based on a negotiated geographical division of its 103 seats between the two parties, the Alliance should consider a unilateral withdrawal from the province in order to leave the field clear for the Tories, cold comfort though that might seem at first blush. But under this scenario, Ontario Alliance supporters and activists, in the spirit of the times, might make the tactical decision to rejoin the federal PC party en masse in order to force a leadership review, to be followed (finally) by serious negotiations with the new leadership of the Alliance.

These talks could then envisage all possibilities, but in view of the time constraints, the simplest arrangement at that point would be a one-time territorial allocation of seats, with the Alliance taking the 91 seats west of Ontario and the renewed PC party taking the rest of the country.

But if our glorious conservative leaders fail Canadians yet again, and none of the above comes to pass, the prospects are truly bleak for our country. It is surely no coincidence that highly-placed Liberals have begun musing in public about the advantages of a common currency, and the need for further integration on various levels with the United States. As they continue to preside complacently over our gradual decline, leading Liberal thinkers are doubtless concluding that the only way to escape the impending disasters predicted by now-Liberal MP John McCallum, among others, is to heed the contention of American journalist and diplomat John Louis O'Sullivan, who in 1845, in relation to the US annexation of Texas, first proclaimed to his countrymen their *"manifest destiny to overspread the continent allotted by Providence for the free development of our yearly multiplying millions."*

There can be no doubt that the slow, almost imperceptible weakening of Canada's relative productivity, our relative standard of living and our dollar, coupled with our significantly higher relative tax burden, contribute to a subtle yet pernicious weakening of our national fabric. These things have the cumulative, insidious effect of sapping our national confidence, even our will to endure as an independent country. Canadians under permanent Liberal rule risk being like the frog in gradually warming water, who doesn't sense that he is being boiled alive until it is too late.

As long as the Canadian Alliance and the Progressive Conservative party remain divided in Parliament, and continue opposing one another electorally in ridings they could otherwise win, the Liberals can, with absolute impunity, treat our very nationhood as their plaything. As the traditional arrogance of the Liberal party in power creeps inevitably back, the rest of us would do well to keep in mind the words of Liberal strongman Clarence Decatur Howe (himself American-born), already referred to. For a split second, during a debate on a government tariff proposal in the House of Commons on May 21, 1951, Howe allowed the Liberal party's mask to slip, revealing its true inner soul. Brushing off the objections of Conservative front-bencher Howard Green (later minister of external affairs in the Diefenbaker government), C.D. Howe blurted out, "Who would stop us? Don't take yourself too seriously. If we wanted to get away with it, who would stop us?" The question is just as relevant today, but much more frightening.

GRITLOCK

Finally, any Alliance or Tory supporter who still believes that no accommodation between the two parties is necessary or possible should consider this: the most likely next act in our political tragedy is the eventual selection by the Liberal party of Paul Martin as their leader. Even if he failed to win a single seat in Western Canada, against a divided opposition the bilingual Mr. Martin could count on at least 50 seats in Quebec and 100 seats in Ontario, plus most of the 32 seats in the Atlantic region — another guaranteed majority Liberal government.

How long must the madness continue?

BACKGROUNDER ONE

Federal Elections Before 1984

IN 1896, AFTER THREE DECADES OF MACDONALD'S TORIES, LAURIER INAUGURATES NINE DECADES OF LIBERAL DOMINANCE BASED ON QUEBEC

In the early years after Confederation in 1867, Canada's Westminster-style two-party system worked reasonably well. Although Sir John A. Macdonald's Tories won six of the seven elections he fought, the Liberal Party was always competitive in every region except little British Columbia, which gave Macdonald its entire six seats through six straight elections. And the Liberals under Alexander Mackenzie actually won the election of 1874 after the Pacific Scandal. The country began with four provinces in 1867, grew to six by the 1872 election, seven by the 1874 election, with the North-West Territories gaining their first representation in the election of 1887; Alberta and Saskatchewan were not carved out of the Territories until 1905. A feature of Macdonald's victories was that he carried Quebec in every election except two: 1874, although he still held on to 30 of Quebec's 65 seats that year, and 1891, when he faced a Liberal leader from Quebec for the one and only time.

Sir John A. died in 1891, two months after winning his final election that year against this new Liberal leader, the young Wilfrid Laurier. Laurier was the first French Canadian to be leader of either major party, and was also Roman Catholic. As a leading Quebec MP, Laurier had already helped the Liberals under Edward Blake win 32 of Quebec's 65 seats in 1887. As party leader in 1891, Laurier had taken 37 Quebec seats against Macdonald's 28. Finally in 1896, against Conservative prime minister Sir Charles Tupper from Nova Scotia, Laurier swept Quebec, 49 to 16, and took 53.5% of Quebec's popular vote, thus beginning his 15-year career as prime minister. Quebec remained faithful to Laurier through the elections of 1900, 1904, 1908, 1911, and 1917, as he consolidated the base of political support that would serve his Liberal Party well until 1984.

Laurier was finally defeated in the so-called Reciprocity Election of 1911. This election saw the emergence of a serious third party for the first time in Canada, as Quebec Nationalist Party leader Henri Bourassa made common cause with the Quebec wing of the Conservatives to oppose Laurier's naval bill. Although Bourassa took 27 Quebec seats and weakened Laurier's hold on Quebec, he did not break it, and the province returned a majority of Liberals, even as the Conservatives under Nova Scotia's Robert Borden swept Ontario. In the wartime conscription election of 1917, Laurier again lost to the victorious Unionist forces under Borden everywhere outside Quebec; but in Quebec, this time with the full support of Bourassa, Laurier still took 62 of the 65 seats and 72.7% of the popular vote.

The election of 1921 saw the first serious threat to the two-party system in Canada, with the emergence of a strong third party outside Quebec, the National Progressive Party or

"Progressives", formed by former Borden minister T.A. Crerar of Manitoba in 1919 after the Borden government failed to reduce tariffs to help farmers. The presence of a large independent third party in the House of Commons gave Canada its first minority governments, in 1921 and 1925, and also produced a House largely divided on regional lines. In 1921, the Progressives put up 148 candidates, and elected 64 members in six provinces, with 23% of the popular vote, while reducing the Conservatives of prime minister Arthur Meighen to 50 seats with 30% of the vote. Mackenzie King's Liberals, one seat short of a majority and with 41% of the vote, were able to govern for four years with the support of Progressive elements when necessary.

By the 1925 election, the Progressives were split, and they ran only 72 candidates in five provinces, electing 24 members in four provinces, with their vote concentrated in the Prairies. This time Meighen's Conservatives won the most seats (116) but not a majority, and King managed to remain in office for eight months with Progressive support, before his ministry resigned in June 1926. In the "King-Byng" election that ensued in September 1926, the Progressives ran only 37 candidates in the same four provinces (Ontario, Manitoba, Saskatchewan and Alberta), and elected 20 members. The Liberals finally secured a majority, with 128 seats out of 245, while the Conservatives held 91 seats. The two-party system had been substantially restored. It is noteworthy that in the three elections of the 1920s which pitted Liberal leader Mackenzie King against Conservative Arthur Meighen, Quebec remained overwhelmingly Liberal, giving the party of Laurier 65, 59 and 60 seats respectively and ensuring King's predominance.

The election of 1930 restored the Conservatives to office after an absence of nine years except for a few months in 1926, this time under the leadership of Calgary lawyer R.B. Bennett. It was to be their last hurrah for the next 27 years. Bennett took 137 seats and 49% of the popular vote, reducing King's Liberals to 91 seats and 45.2% of the vote. The Progressives hung on with 12 seats, 9 of which were in Alberta, but were no longer a serious factor. The most encouraging feature of the 1930 election for the Conservatives was a significant breakthrough in Quebec, where they took 24 of the 65 seats and an amazing 44.7% of the popular vote. There were a number of reasons that converged to produce this surprising performance, the Tories' best unaided Quebec result since 1891, but no single cause that might have provided a lasting foundation for future success. But unquestionably Bennett benefited from the presence of a still relatively strong provincial Conservative Party in Quebec, which, although in opposition to the Quebec Liberal regime of premier Alexandre Taschereau, was nevertheless able to exploit the weaknesses of the federal Liberals, thanks to the strong leadership of Arthur Sauvé.

In 1935, King returned in triumph, to remain prime minister until his retirement in late 1948. This time, the vagaries of our electoral system gave his Liberal Party 173 seats with 44.8% of the popular vote (lower than in 1930), reducing Bennett's Conservatives to a mere 40 seats despite their receiving almost 30% of the vote. Twenty-five of the Tory seats were in Ontario (as also in 1940). This election saw the emergence of three new parties: the socialist Co-operative Commonwealth Federation (CCF) under J.S. Woodsworth of North Winnipeg, running on its Regina Manifesto of 1933; the Reconstruction Party led by rebel Tory H.H. Stevens of British Columbia, formed at the last minute to run against big business; and the Social Credit Party, a federal offshoot of William Aberhart's just-elected Social Credit League in Alberta. In Canada's 245 seats, the CCF ran 118 candidates and elected seven of them with 8.8% of the popular vote; the Reconstructionists ran 174 candidates, electing only Stevens himself, but taking 8.7% of the popular vote; while Social Credit ran 45 candidates, mostly in Alberta and Saskatchewan, electing 17 members in those two provinces with only 4.1% of the national vote. Quebec returned solidly to the Liberal fold, giving King 55 Liberals and five Independent Liberals, while the Conservatives were once again reduced to five English-speaking members in the province, with 28.2% of the popular vote.

In the 1940 election, early in the war, King did even better than his 1935 landslide, winning 181 seats against 40 for the Conservatives under Dr. R.J. Manion of Ontario, who had been chosen leader in July 1938 following Bennett's resignation in March. Manion, an ex-Liberal Irish Catholic with a French-Canadian wife, was defeated in Fort William, and led his party backward in Quebec, where Gaspé returned the sole Conservative (and an Independent Conservative at that) thanks to a division in the Liberal vote. The CCF, now led by Woodsworth and M.J. Coldwell, its national chairman, elected just eight members among its 96 candidates.

The Reconstruction Party had disappeared, Stevens having rejoined the Conservatives, but another renegade Tory, R.B. Bennett's brother-in-law W.D. Herridge, had launched the New Democracy movement in 1939, and teamed up with Social Credit for the election. Together, they elected 10 members, all in Alberta, from their total of 29 candidates. Quebec, of course, returned 61 Liberals and three Independent Liberals, reducing the Tories to 19.8% of the popular vote as against the Liberals' 63.3%. One might say that by this point, Canada's party system was no longer one in which two national parties might alternate in power, but had become a system of one national governing party and one national opposition party, with two small region-alized third parties. It stayed that way until 1957; but at least the Conservatives stayed firmly (if distantly) in second place, and were never dislodged from this dubious honour by any of the third parties throughout this period.

By the time of the 1945 election, Mackenzie King had successfully survived the war and its attendant conscription crises. The Conservatives, whose official name from 1920 to 1940 had been "National Liberal and Conservative", had in 1940 changed their name to "National Conservative", although Manion's candidates had run that year under the banner of "National Government". Then, in late 1942, after choosing as their new leader John Bracken, the Progressive premier of Manitoba since 1920, they changed their name yet again, this time to "Progressive Conservative". But King knew this was all window dressing, and that his main threat could well come from the CCF, who, like Labour in Britain, were proposing dramatic new social measures. So King stole their thunder by introducing family allowances in early 1944. He also proposed minimum standards of nutrition and housing, and insurance against unemployment, accident, ill health and old age. The CCF under M.J. Coldwell presented 205 candidates, one more than the Progressive Conservatives, and elected 28 members, 18 of them in Saskatchewan (beating the prime minister in Prince Albert), and taking 15.6% of the popular vote. Social Credit, backed by premier Ernest Manning, took 13 seats, all in Alberta. Bracken's Tories improved their position to 67 seats, 48 of which were in Ontario. But King won his third consecutive majority with 125 seats out of 245, thanks to holding 53 seats in Quebec. In that province, the nationalist Bloc Populaire, although electing only two members, cut deeply into the already low Tory vote, reducing it to a historic minimum up to that time of only 8.4%, yielding two seats. Yet the Progressive Conservatives, like the victorious Liberals, still managed to retain representation in every province.

King finally retired in 1948 and was succeeded by Quebec's Louis St. Laurent, his minister of justice. In the 1949 election, St. Laurent coasted to an easy victory against new Tory leader George Drew, the former premier of Ontario (1943-48). He did much the same again four years later, in the election of 1953.

There were a number of features common to both of these elections. The Liberals got secure majorities (193 and 171 seats respectively) with just under half the popular vote, and all but a few of Quebec's seats. They beat the Tories in every province, but the Tories still won seats in every province except for Newfoundland in 1953. Of the Tories' 41 seats in 1949, and 51 in 1953, about four fifths came from Ontario each time. The Tory popular vote nationwide was 29.7% in 1949 and 31% in 1953.

In each election, the CCF came third (13 mainly western seats in 1949, 23 in 1953) and Social Credit came fourth (10 Alberta seats in 1949, and 11 in 1953, plus four more in W.A.C. Bennett's British Columbia for a total of 15). Quebec premier Maurice Duplessis, no friend of the Liberals, allowed his Union Nationale organization to support Quebec Tory candidates, without risking his personal prestige on a lost cause. This gave the Conservatives 24.5% of Quebec's popular vote in 1949 and 29.4% in 1953, but only two and four seats respectively.

The Liberals had now won five elections in a row, a feat never achieved by Macdonald, and had confirmed their pattern of alternating their leaders from Ontario (Blake and King, both unilingual) and Quebec (Laurier and St. Laurent, both perfectly bilingual). The Progressive Conservatives, like the small back wheel on a penny-farthing bicycle, trailed reliably along behind.

But at least in those days, the Liberal government could not last forever. George Drew retired in 1956, and was replaced as Conservative leader by the unilingual John Diefenbaker, a long-time MP from Saskatchewan (he was supported at the convention by a young delegate named Brian Mulroney). St. Laurent was 75 when he called the 1957 election, and Diefenbaker succeeded in portraying the Liberal team as arrogant and out of touch. The Conservatives increased their popular vote to 38.9% compared to 40.9% for the Liberals. They were able to capitalize on their long-standing number two position in most ridings by picking up 61 new seats, 56 outside Quebec and five in Quebec (for a total of nine, and 31.1% of the vote) with Union Nationale help. This gave them 112 seats, representing every province, to the Liberals' 105, from all except PEI. Native son St. Laurent held 62 Quebec seats, but these were offset by 61 Tory seats in Ontario. Both the CCF and Social Credit improved their standings slightly, to 25 and 19 seats respectively. St. Laurent resigned, and Diefenbaker formed a minority government. After 22 years, the Conservatives were back in power.

Diefenbaker moved quickly to implement the most elec-torally appealing elements of his program, and hoped for an opportunity to dissolve the House. It came after Louis St. Laurent retired, and was replaced as Liberal leader by Lester B. Pearson of Ontario, the former minister of external affairs whose French was only marginally better than Diefenbaker's. Pearson called on the government to resign, and Diefenbaker responded by calling an election for March 31, 1958, not ten months after the previous one. It produced the greatest sweep in Canadian history, giving Diefenbaker 53.6% of the popular vote and 208 seats out of 265. The Liberals were reduced to 49 seats and 33.6%, while the CCF fell to eight seats and Social Credit was wiped out. Diefenbaker took every seat in Nova Scotia, PEI, Manitoba and Alberta, while the Liberals' only seat west of Ontario was the North-West

Territories. But the biggest news was in Quebec, where the absence of a French-Canadian party leader left a political void which the Liberals could no longer fill. In rushed the Conservatives, this time with Premier Duplessis' active behind-the-scenes support, taking 50 of the province's 75 seats and 49.6% of its popular vote — a level not seen since 1887 — against the Liberals' 45.7%. But it was not to last.

The messianic qualities that made Diefenbaker such a formidable campaigner were not matched by the managerial ability needed to run the country, and many of his supporters of 1958 soon concluded that their idol had feet of clay. Meanwhile, the CCF changed its name to the New Democratic Party and chose former Saskatchewan premier T.C. Douglas as leader, while Social Credit turned to Robert Thompson of Alberta as national leader and Quebec's Réal Caouette as "associate leader". In Quebec, after Duplessis' death in 1959, the Union Nationale was beaten by the Liberals under Jean Lesage. In the 1962 election, it was perhaps Caouette's presence as a home-grown Quebec leader that did Diefenbaker the most damage. Caouette's "Créditistes" came from nowhere to take 26 Quebec seats with 26% of the vote, while helping through vote-splitting to bring the Liberal total up to 35 seats with only 39.2%. The Conservatives fell back to 14 seats, with 29.6%.

In four years, Diefenbaker had lost 36 Quebec seats, even more than the 32 seats he lost in Ontario. He was reduced to a minority, with 37.3% of the popular vote, and governed for nine months with 116 members out of 265. Pearson's Liberals had 100 seats and 37.2%, the NDP 19 seats and 13.5%, and Social Credit 30 seats and 11.7%. The Liberals took seats in every province except PEI and Alberta.

Diefenbaker's minority government fell on February 5, 1963, and the same leaders confronted each other in the 1963 election as in 1962. The result was yet another minority government, but this time a Liberal one. Pearson got 129 seats with 41.7% of the popular vote, while Diefenbaker dropped to 95 seats with 32.8%. Desperate for a majority, Pearson called a third election in four years in 1965, but could win only another minority — 131 seats versus the Conservatives' 97, and only 40.2% of the popular vote, while the Tories dropped slightly to 32.4%. In 1963 and 1965, the NDP took 17 and 21 seats respectively, while Social Credit and their Créditiste cousins in Quebec took 24 and 14, as Caouette faded to only nine seats in 1965. Meanwhile, the Conservatives held on to eight Quebec seats in each election, with 19.5% and 21.3% of the popular vote respectively. In both elections, the Conservatives won seats in every province except Newfoundland, whereas in 1965 the Liberals had no seats in three provinces: PEI, Saskatchewan, and Alberta.

By this time, the country was largely sick of the Diefenbaker-Pearson rivalry, and both major parties were ready for new leaders. The Conservatives moved first, choosing essentially unilingual Nova Scotia premier Robert Stanfield in September 1967, with the Liberals following in April 1968. Their choice was a swinging bachelor intellectual, the perfectly bilingual Pierre Elliott Trudeau from Montreal, who had served briefly as Pearson's minister of justice. In the election of June 1968, Trudeau dazzled the media of Toronto, Vancouver and Montreal, and the Liberals finally managed to win a majority of 155 seats, including 64 in Ontario and 16 in British Columbia, with 45.5% of the national vote. They took seats in every province except PEI, and would have swept Quebec *à la* Laurier or St. Laurent, had it not been for the surprising resurgence of Réal Caouette (surreptitiously assisted in some seats by the Union Nationale). As it was, they took 56 of Quebec's 74 seats, with 53.6% of the popular vote, while the Ralliement des Créditistes took 14 rural seats with only 16.4%, leaving just four seats for Stanfield's Tories, who nevertheless took 21.3% of the votes.

Stanfield took all but seven of the 32 Atlantic seats, most astonishingly winning six in the Liberal bastion of Newfoundland, but managed only 17 Ontario seats (the Tories' lowest ever at that point) and 26 seats in the West, for a national total of 72 seats and 31.4% of the vote. Yet he still had representation in every province but one, British Columbia, where the NDP took seven of its national total of 22 seats. Social Credit, by now divorced from the Créditistes, ran 31 candidates outside Quebec but elected none, and disappeared as a federal political force in English-speaking Canada. The two-party system was still alive in Canada, although weakened by a western-based socialist party that got 17% of the national vote and a protest party confined to Quebec.

Stanfield's Tories made a major comeback in the election of 1972, but not quite enough to unseat an over-complacent Trudeau, who had campaigned on the uninspiring slogan "The land is strong". The Trudeaumania of 1968 was definitely dead in English-speaking Canada, but once again Quebec salvaged a minority government for the Liberals. Stanfield got 36% of the popular vote and won seats in every province, including all 19 seats in Alberta, finishing at 107 seats, a heartbreaking two seats below the Liberal total of 109. The Liberal popular vote dropped seven points to 38.5%. With a new leader in David Lewis of Ontario, the NDP took 17.7% and gained nine seats for a historic high of 31, while the Créditistes gained one seat from the Tories to reach 15. Quebec gave 49.1% of its votes to the Liberals, for 56 seats as in 1968, representing over half their caucus. The Créditistes came next with 24.4%, and the Tories a dismal third with only 17.4% and two seats. Stanfield actually took more seats than Trudeau in every province except two: New

Brunswick, where they tied at five each, and Quebec. It seemed that Canada's regional cleavages were making short-term minority governments the rule, and majorities the exception.

But in 1974, Trudeau did regain a majority, with 141 seats out of 264 and 43.2% of the popular vote, by dint of a strong upsurge in Ontario. There he rose to 55 seats, up from 36 two years earlier. Stanfield got 95 seats and 35.4% of the vote, while the NDP were reduced to 16 seats and the Créditistes to 11. Once again, the Tories were the only party with seats in every province, but still they were routed in Quebec where the Liberals took 60 seats and 54.1% of the vote to their three seats and 21.2%. At least the Tories finished ahead of the Créditistes at 17.1%, but the Liberals continued to be the major beneficiaries of the Créditistes' gradual decline.

By 1979, the Trudeau government was thoroughly unpopular, and the prime minister waited until almost the last possible moment before calling the election. In 1976, Joe Clark had replaced Stanfield as Conservative leader, and he capitalized on the general discontent in English-speaking Canada by winning 136 seats to the Liberals' 114 and the NDP's 26, enough for a convincing minority government. The Conservatives were back in office, this time after an absence of only 16 years, in contrast to their previous drought of 22 years.

Clark, an Albertan who was functionally bilingual, did particularly well in Ontario, taking 57 seats to the Liberals' 32 and the NDP's six; but the Liberals countered with 67 seats in Quebec as the Créditistes sank back to six and the Tories stayed at two. Owing to their Quebec strength, the Liberals won the national popular vote with 40.1%, compared to 35.9% for the Tories and 17.9% for the NDP. In Quebec, the Liberals took 61.7% and the Tories only 13.5%, while the Créditiste decline continued to 16%. This time, the Liberals were completely shut out of three provinces: Alberta, Saskatchewan and PEI, while the Tories, although severely under-represented in Quebec, had seats in all provinces.

Following his defeat by Clark, Trudeau announced his retirement, and the Liberal party began preparations for a leadership convention. But to general astonishment, the Clark government was defeated in the House of Commons on its first budget, when it neglected to secure the support of Réal Caouette's six Créditiste members, and the leaderless Liberals were suddenly on the verge of an election caused by their budget vote. They persuaded a sceptical Trudeau that he could win, and he came out of retirement to lead his party to a clear majority in the 1980 election. He gained 33 seats, including 20 in Ontario and seven in Quebec, for a total of 147, while Clark dropped back to 103. The NDP under Ed Broadbent gained six seats for a new high of 32, while the Créditistes were finally wiped out and eliminated from the House of Commons.

For the first election since 1958, only three parties were now represented in the House. This time, the eastern concentration of Liberal support was even more pronounced, as the Liberals had not a single seat in the three western provinces and the territories, and only two seats in Manitoba. On the other hand, they took 74 of Quebec's 75 seats, leaving the Tories with only one; but the Tories could still claim to have seats in every province. Skewed once again by Quebec, the national popular vote was 44.3% Liberal, 32.5% PC, and 19.8% NDP. In Quebec, it was 68.2% Liberal, 12.6% PC, 9.1% NDP (another historic high, but no cigar), and 5.9% Créditiste.

Federal Elections from 1984 to 1997

FORMATION AND DESTRUCTION OF THE "MULRONEY COALITION" OF QUEBEC AND ALBERTA, 1984-1993; RISE OF REFORM AND THE BLOC QUÉBÉCOIS; END OF THE TWO-PARTY SYSTEM IN 1993, LEADING TO LIBERAL HEGEMONY

When Quebecer Brian Mulroney won the leadership of the Progressive Conservative party from Joe Clark in 1983, Quebecer Pierre Trudeau was still prime minister. Given Trudeau's 74 Quebec seats, and the Liberal party's utter dependence on Quebec as the virtually impregnable foundation of its parliamentary pluralities ever since 1896, there was a tantalizing possibility that, for the first time in Canadian history, our two major parties could enter an election with each led by a bilingual Quebecer.

Whenever they had been given the opportunity, francophones in Quebec and elsewhere had always voted massively for parties that were led by fellow francophones. Since, of the two national parties, only the Liberals had ever had any francophone leaders (Laurier, St. Laurent, and now Trudeau), they had been the major beneficiaries of this truism, and they had built their political success on it for almost nine decades. But Réal Caouette had proved that the formula could work for other parties (as Lucien Bouchard was later to confirm).

After countless defeats caused by a Liberal Quebec, the Tories seemed to have finally caught on. But political junkies were denied the dream match — the Quebecers' *mano-a-mano* that we still have yet to see — when Trudeau took his "walk in the snow" and decided to retire, this time for good.

1) The 1984 election: Mulroney's record landslide

Trudeau was succeeded by former cabinet minister John Turner, who, although he had cut his political teeth in Montreal, was now based in Vancouver. Turner was neither as bilingual nor as *québécois* as Mulroney, thus leaving the boy from Baie Comeau an open run at the Liberals' traditional Quebec base, where they had won 74 of the 75 seats in 1980. Mulroney was not slow to seize his opportunity, and in the election that Turner soon called for September 1984, the Conservatives took 58 of Quebec's 75 seats — an even better score than Diefenbaker's 50 seats against Pearson in 1958. In terms of the percentage of Quebec's seats (77%) taken by a Conservative, even Macdonald had only surpassed this achievement once, when he took 51 of the 65 Quebec seats in 1882 (78.5%).

And in terms of the swing in Quebec's popular vote from 1980 to 1984, the figures were astonishing and unprecedented: the Liberals' popular vote dropped 26.3 points, from 61.7% to 35.4%, their lowest in history to that point, while the Conservative vote rose 36.7 points, from 13.5% to 50.2%. In the 1988 election, Mulroney did even better in Quebec. What more dramatic proof can there be of the massive predisposition of Quebecers to vote for one of their own? In the event, the Liberal party was to be denied its traditional electoral pre-eminence in Quebec for an unprecedented five straight elections.

Having successfully stolen the Liberals' Quebec base, all Mulroney needed to do to win a majority was retain his own party's base in Western Canada, secured initially by John Diefenbaker, and held by Stanfield and Clark, and garner at least the traditionally Tory seats in Ontario and the Atlantic. This he did in spades, winning the largest number of seats — 211 — ever taken by one party in Canadian history. He won 58 of 77 western seats — all 21 in Alberta and 19 out of 28 in British Columbia — and 67 of 95 seats in Ontario. He won 25 of the 32 seats in the Atlantic provinces, beating the Liberals handily in every province and territory in the country.

Although reduced to 40 seats, of which 17 were in Quebec, the Liberal party was not dead. It still had seats in every province except Alberta and Saskatchewan, Turner having brought his party back to British Columbia by winning his own riding of Vancouver Quadra in a tough fight. Interestingly, the NDP largely resisted the Tory tide, electing 30 members as opposed to 32 in 1980, and actually benefitting from the Liberal decline in Ontario by picking up eight new seats there. As for the national popular vote, the Conservatives got 50%, the Liberals 28%, and the NDP 18.9%.

Mulroney was soon beset by the political reverses that always seem to follow such a lopsided victory. His popularity ebbed and flowed, and he succeeded in keeping the Liberal Party largely at bay during his first term. But he did not foresee, or at least he did not forestall, the rise of the two political movements — essentially the work of two men — that would eventually destroy his party, Canada's historic party of Confederation, and with it, any vestige of a two-party system in Canada.

2) The rise of the Reform Party of Canada

The first of these movements was the Reform Party, started in Vancouver by Preston Manning and Stan Roberts as the Reform Association of Canada, in May 1987. As a young man, Manning had co-written a book with his father, Social Credit premier Ernest C. Manning of Alberta, entitled *Political Realignment: A Challenge to Thoughtful Canadians*, published in 1967. Concluding that the ideological realignment he and his father were calling for could only be realized in reaction to an (inevitably) imperfectly pure Conservative government, Manning waited until 1986 before starting his movement in earnest.

The Reform agenda was a natural continuation of the prairie populist movements of the past, advocating referenda, plebiscites, recall, free votes in Parliament, and above all, Senate reform. The western-based party was to be economically and socially conservative, and anti-socialist. It would exploit issues on which it could accuse the Conservatives of being too left-wing, such as the public debt and annual government deficits, privatization, and deregulation of enterprise on the economic side, and on the social policy side, bilingualism and biculturalism, the death penalty, abortion, family values, and other moral issues.

Western discontent with Ottawa, always present no matter which party Central Canada votes into office, was easy to inflame over such issues as patronage, the decline of the B.C. and Alberta economies, the too-slow removal of the Petroleum and Gas Revenue Tax (repealed in 1987), and the 1986 budget's lack of support for agriculture, the Husky Oil Upgrader at Lloydminster, or the Syncrude plant at Fort McMurray. Perhaps the last straw was the perceived unfairness of awarding the CF-18 maintenance contract in the fall of 1986 to Canadair-CAE in Montreal (now Bombardier) instead of to low-bidder Bristol Aerospace of Winnipeg. No matter that this strengthened a then nascent and now thriving Canadian industry instead of a British-owned branch plant, to Western Canadians it was final proof of Mulroney's long-suspected favouritism towards his native Quebec and disregard of their own interests.

The Reform Association became the Reform Party of Canada at a founding convention in Winnipeg in the fall of 1987, attended by 140 Albertans, 91 British Columbians, 65 Manitobans, and 10 Saskatchewan representatives — 306 in all. The convention chose Preston Manning as leader after his only rival, co-founder Stan Roberts, withdrew, accusing Manning's supporters of various irregularities and prejudices.

In the 1988 election one year later, Reform contested only 72 ridings, all in the West — 30 in British Columbia, all 26 of Alberta's seats, 4 in Saskatchewan, and 12 in Manitoba. Although they elected no members, their popular vote in these contested ridings ranged from a high of 33.3% to a low of 0.9%, for an average of 8.5% in all 72 ridings. Although few Tories realized it at the time, Reform and Manning were on their way to supplanting them in Western Canada.

3) The 1988 election: free trade saves the Mulroney government

Mulroney made the 1988 election a virtual national referendum on the North American Free Trade Agreement, and a Quebec referendum on the 1987 Meech Lake Accord, although regional frustrations with his government inevitably played a role.

With Reform not yet a serious threat, the Tories were able to hold 48 of their 58 seats in Western Canada, including 25 seats in Alberta. Redistribution had added 13 new seats to the House, including four in British Columbia and five in Alberta, thereby raising the western regional total to 86 seats plus three in the territories. While the Liberals could make no gains in the two westernmost provinces, holding only Turner's Vancouver seat and still being excluded from Alberta, it was the NDP that took away Tory seats, winning a surprising 19 seats in B.C. and an even more surprising one seat in Alberta! The Liberals did pick up four seats in Manitoba, even taking two away from the NDP, although they still could not break into Saskatchewan, where the NDP took 10 seats. Mulroney suffered major losses to the Liberals in Ontario (a decline from 67 to 46 seats) and in the Atlantic, where the Liberals gained 13 seats to carry the region by 20 seats to 12. But he actually gained five seats in Quebec, bringing his total to a Trudeauesque 63, and humbling the Liberal party to a miserable 12 Montreal-area seats.

The end result was 169 seats for Mulroney, his second consecutive majority (a feat not accomplished by any Tory since Macdonald), 83 seats for the Liberals (but still none in two provinces), and a remarkable 43 seats for the NDP, in five provinces plus the Yukon. The popular vote went 42.9% for the Conservatives and 32% for the Liberals, with the NDP taking their highest figure ever at 20.4%. In Quebec, the Tories took a record 52.7% of the vote, the Liberals 30.3%, and the NDP a record 14%.

Mulroney had confirmed his appropriation of the Liberals' classic formula for victory: an overwhelming Quebec base, supplemented by competitive showings in the other regions of the country. But just as Diefenbaker had been unable to consolidate his great breakthrough in Quebec, so did Mulroney's success fail to outlast his own leadership; and in both cases, it was mainly an unsuspected new third party that seduced the Conservative vote away.

As for Alberta, the second pillar of his electoral coalition, a premonition of things to come was the by-election of March 13, 1989 in the riding of Beaver River, won handily by

Deborah Grey who thus became Reform's first elected MP. Mulroney also gave Reform a great public relations weapon by initially refusing to appoint to an Alberta vacancy in the Senate the landslide winner of a provincially-sponsored election for that purpose on October 16, 1989, Reform Party candidate Stan Waters. Eight months later, on June 11, 1990, Mulroney finally agreed to appoint Waters, in return for Alberta Premier Donald Getty's support during the first ministers' talks on the Meech Lake Accord earlier that month, but the damage was already done.

4) The rise of the Bloc Québécois

The other new political movement that would help destroy Mulroney's coalition was the Bloc Québécois. The Bloc was a direct outgrowth of the complex and painful final agonies of the Meech Lake Accord, which need not be explored in detail here. Suffice it to say that Lucien Bouchard used the excuse of the report of a parliamentary committee on the Accord chaired by Jean Charest, which was tabled in the House of Commons on May 17, 1990, to resign dramatically from the Mulroney government and the Conservative party five days later, on May 22. (His resignation had been preceded on May 18 by that of François Gérin, the somewhat more impetuous MP from Megantic-Compton-Stanstead.)

According to the late Mordecai Richler, Bouchard, the most nationalist and ambitious of Mulroney's Quebec ministers, had told reporters as early as the spring of 1989 — when Meech was already in trouble in two provinces — that if the Accord did not pass, he would have to re-evaluate his position in federal politics. Jacques Parizeau, leader of the opposition in Quebec, had also said that his Parti Québécois would welcome any and all disillusioned Quebec MPs. Bouchard, now sitting as an independent, was followed the same day by Gilbert Chartrand, Tory member for Verdun-St. Paul.

On June 26, three more Quebec Tory backbenchers resigned from their caucus to protest the death of Meech on June 23, while the Liberal member for Shefford, Jean Lapierre, left his caucus the same day to protest the first-ballot election of Jean Chrétien as Liberal leader, which had also occurred on June 23. Lapierre was followed on July 3 by Gilles Rocheleau, Liberal member for Hull, who denounced Chrétien as responsible for the death of Meech. Bouchard, spokesman for the eight sovereignist Quebec MPs now sitting as independents, said that they had agreed not to form an official party, but wished to be known as the Bloc Québécois in the House of Commons. On August 12, Gilles Duceppe, running as an independent affiliated with the Bloc, easily won a by-election in the Montreal riding of Laurier-Sainte Marie. But on February 11, 1991, the Bloc did apply for official party status, as polls indicated that it could win 60 of Quebec's 75 seats. Bouchard's brilliant and opportunistic exploitation of the death of the Meech Lake Accord had struck Conservative support in Quebec a mortal blow, as the next election would soon confirm.

5) The 1993 election: the annihilation of the Progressive Conservative Party ends Canada's two-party system, ensuring Liberal governments by default

The stage was now set for the 1993 election, which would prove catastrophic both for the venerable Progressive Conservative Party of Canada and for Canadian democracy. Mulroney attempted to salvage the ruins of Meech through the Charlottetown Accord, which was put to a national referendum on October 26, 1992. After some hesitation, Manning opposed the Accord, as did Bouchard, Parizeau, and a motley crew of incompatible interests (including Trudeau), and it went down to defeat by a 54% vote for the No side. It lost in every western province, as well as in Quebec.

In February 1993, the now unpopular Mulroney announced his retirement, and he was succeeded in June by British Columbia's intelligent, functionally bilingual Kim Campbell, who found herself facing not one but two party leaders from Quebec (Chrétien and Bouchard), as well as Manning from Alberta. After a promising summer, on September 8, Campbell called an election for October 25, 1993. But the tide immediately turned against the Tories with Campbell's opening press conference, when she opined that Canadians could expect no relief from unemployment until at least the year 2000; her campaign went downhill from there, error piling upon error, through seven long weeks. Tory support in the polls plunged from 36%, to 30%, to 22%, while Campbell's own approval rating fell from 51% in August to just 17% by election day. Meanwhile, the Bloc Québécois continued to rise in Quebec, Reform advanced strongly in British Columbia and Alberta, and the NDP (under new leader Audrey McLaughlin) collapsed everywhere. All Chrétien needed to do was to appear competent and statesmanlike.

The resulting implosion of the Conservative party surpassed anything in Canadian history. Harried and scavenged from three sides, led by a neophyte with no national campaign experience and virtually no program, it was utterly destroyed as a national force, and like Caesar's Gaul, its domains were divided into three parts. The western part went to Manning's Reform, which took 52 seats, including 24 in British Columbia, 22 in Alberta, and four in Saskatchewan. The eastern part, Quebec (the Atlantic had already gone substantially Liberal in 1988), went mainly to Bouchard's Bloc Québécois, whose 54 seats were enough to edge out Reform as the Official Opposition. And the central part, Ontario, in a sweep never remotely approached before, went overwhelmingly to Chrétien's Liberals, as they took 98 of its 99 seats (Reform got the other one). The Liberals also took 12 of Manitoba's 14 seats, giving them total domination of the two mid-Canadian provinces, and 31 of the 32 seats in the four Atlantic provinces. With 19 seats in Quebec (seven more than in 1988), the Liberals easily formed a majority government, with 177 seats nationally. The NDP fell from their historic high of 43 seats in 1988 to an historic low of nine seats in 1993, thereby losing official party status.

But even that result was better than the Tories', who managed to salvage only Jean Charest's seat in Sherbrooke, Quebec, and Elsie Wayne's in Saint John, New Brunswick. Having lost her own seat, Kim Campbell resigned as leader, and was succeeded by Charest.

A fascinating feature of federal elections in Ontario, which helps to explain the three Liberal sweeps of the province since 1993, has been the effect of the precipitous drop in support for the NDP after the departure of Ontarian Ed Broadbent, that party's most successful leader. In 1993, the NDP lost over two-thirds of their traditional Ontario support to the Liberals, thereby destroying the three-way balance of power that had prevailed for many years. In 1988, the Liberals had taken 38.9% of Ontario's votes, and the NDP 20.1%, for a combined total of 59%.

This combined total has hardly changed in the three subsequent elections (58.8%, 60.2%, 59.8%), but in 1993, the Liberal component of it jumped 14 points to 52.9%, while the NDP component fell by the same 14 points to 6%. This increase in the Liberal popular vote to over half the Ontario total has been sufficient to earn them virtually every Ontario seat for three elections running.

Just as the combined Liberal/NDP vote has remained constant for four elections at around 60%, the combined PC/Reform/Alliance vote has also remained constant since 1988 at around 38% (38.2%, 37.7%, 38.9% and 38%). But the fact that, since the advent of Reform in 1993, this 38% has been more or less evenly split between two parties, instead of all going to the Tories as in 1988, has meant a subsequent dearth of Ontario seats for either party. The good news for small-c conservatives in Ontario is that much of the 60% that seems arrayed against them is over-concentrated in urban ridings, with the balance actually much more equal in many non-urban ridings. They should also recognize that if they can ever present Ontario voters with a single, credible united front, their 38% share might increase substantially; in 1984, for example, the PC party, at that time alone on its side of the fence, got 47.6% of Ontario's votes, good for 67 seats.

As well as causing the virtual disappearance of the Conservative party, the 1993 election was unique in three other respects. For the first time in history, the Liberal party under a Quebec francophone leader failed to dominate Quebec, as Chrétien got only 19 seats and 33% of the vote, against 54 seats and 49.3% of the vote for Bouchard, while Campbell (or perhaps Charest) took 13.5% of the vote for the single Tory seat. The second unique feature, already mentioned, was the unprecedented Liberal sweep of Ontario, where the fortuitous collapse of the NDP and presence of two conservative parties gave Chrétien a new Liberal power-base, in compensation for the old Quebec base he could not reconquer.

And the final point, which cannot be overemphasized, was the end of Canada's two-party system which, though imperfect, had facilitated at least the occasional victory of the second national party over the first. For the first time in

Canadian history, while the governing party held seats in every province (the Liberals finally took four seats in Alberta and five in Saskatchewan), no other party had seats in more than five provinces. To all intents and purposes, Reform was a purely western party, the NDP a Saskatchewan party with a B.C. branch, and the Tories an eastern rump, while the Bloc Québécois never pretended any interest beyond Quebec. For the first time in 126 years, Canada had only one national party. In hindsight, it should not have been difficult to foretell the future electoral consequences of this new but fundamental defect in our democracy.

The following two charts graphically illustrate the collapse of Canada's two-party system in 1993, and the dominance of a single party ever since. The first chart shows the rise and fall in levels of public support for the Liberal and (Progressive) Conservative parties only, for all federal elections from 1891 (Macdonald's last victory) to 2000. For well over 100 years before 1993, both these parties could claim to have truly national support. The second chart adds the three other parties represented in the House of Commons today, but only from the 1984 election (Mulroney's first victory) to 2000.

Liberal and (Progressive) Conservative popular vote, Canadian federal elections 1891-2000

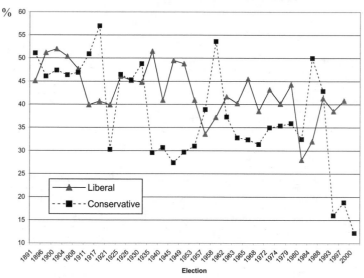

Popular vote for five parliamentary parties, Canadian federal elections 1984-2000

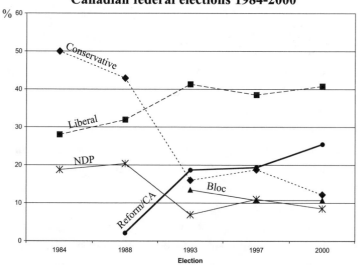

6) The demonization of Mulroney and Manning

The only way that most Canadians can form a personal impression of our political leaders is from reports, images and opinions in the media, and to a lesser extent from the views of our friends and co-workers, which are also largely formed by the media. Very few of us have the opportunity to know a leader personally. There is nothing new about this. But a significant change from, say, the years of St. Laurent, Drew and Woodsworth, has been the ever-increasing intensity of media scrutiny in the television age, the ever-greater focus on the persona of the leader, and the artificial reductionism necessitated by the shorter and shorter "sound bites" that TV news directors accord politicians today. An early victim of this trend was Conservative leader Robert Stanfield, who complained in 1968, "You walk out (of the House) and they shove a bunch of microphones in your face and in 30 seconds you're expected to produce a profound and intelligent answer to … an extremely complicated national issue." Today it would be eight seconds.

Our politics have become the politics of image more than substance, and the effective creation and manipulation of each competing leader's image is now absolutely critical to their success or failure. The old concept of "charisma", as attributed to Kennedy, Diefenbaker and Trudeau, has been further refined by the image makers, so that today a politician's image is made up of an amalgam of "positives" and "negatives" — or "favourables" and "unfavourables" — each of which is carefully measured by the party pollster, and then further manipulated by the media advisers to produce the best possible effect, given the raw material available.

But in analyzing the effect on voter behaviour of the several components of a politician's image, US election specialists discovered that it was far easier to persuade people to vote *against* a person, by portraying the candidate in a negative light, than it was to persuade them to vote *for* someone. This is due to the well-known fact that most of us are more inclined to believe negative information about a person than positive claims — in the age of advertising, we are automatically suspicious of hype, and we are particularly cynical about politicians.

One hugely important consequence of this new sophistication, still little understood by the general public, is the electoral campaign method of concentrating more and more on destroying the image of your opponent, rather than improving your own. This is known as "driving up your opponent's negatives", and the slogan "Go negative!" has become a byword among American consultants, who are by far the most experienced electoral manipulators in the world. Character assassination has become the order of the day, although it is euphemistically called "defining your opponent's image" by the experts. And whatever one may think of this practice, the incontrovertible fact is that it works.

The primary vehicle for it is paid TV ads, although the real pros are very good at getting free negative media about their opponents by "spinning" selected reporters and editors — many of whom are happy to participate in the manipulation, particularly if it matches their own biases. Many in the media also love the sense of power that comes with helping to manipulate the outcome of an election behind the scenes, safe from excessive scrutiny. As British prime minister Stanley Baldwin observed about Canadian-born press magnate Lord Beaverbrook in a speech in London on March 18, 1931 — having borrowed the phrase from its originator, author Rudyard Kipling — the media have "power without responsibility: the prerogative of the harlot throughout the ages."

As negative advertising took hold in the 1970s and 1980s, many US election contests became mudslinging battles, where the winners were the candidates best able to pin credible charges on their opponents, while deflecting attacks on themselves. In 1983 Ronald Reagan acquired the sobriquet "the Teflon president", because nothing would stick to him — and he is also an object lesson in the importance of an aura of decency, innocence, and sincerity, as compared to Nixon's image of deviousness and trickery. Canada's Liberal Party, never slow to import a good idea, soon understood the value of the new American techniques and began experimenting with them. As the political joke goes, all you really need to succeed in politics is sincerity — and if you can fake that, you've got it made.

Although one can only conjecture at the inner schemes of Liberal strategists, it would not be far wrong to date a change in tone from the election of Jean Chrétien as Liberal leader in June, 1990. Brian Mulroney, as the Liberals' main opponent at the time, was their first target and victim. Coinciding with the death of the Meech Lake Accord, the advent of a new team of strategists long associated with Chrétien seemed to bring a harsher approach to the denigration of Mulroney's image, and he was soon being routinely called "the most hated prime minister in Canadian history".

What little civility had prevailed in federal politics while Turner was Liberal leader now seemed to evaporate, as the Chrétien team knew that the key to victory was to make Mulroney, after two majority governments, seem terminally unacceptable to Canadian voters. They calculated that his greatest weakness was what came to be known as the "sleaze factor", and hammered at it ruthlessly. The strategy of magnifying Mulroney's faults and minimizing his achievements was so effective that even today — eight years and three elections after he retired — his memory is still reviled by many Canadians, and his significant achievements largely unappreciated.

Since it is the victors who influence the writing of history, Mulroney has not been well treated by most journalists subsequent to 1993. The most blatant example of the vilification of his reputation, as mentioned in the first chapter, is Stevie Cameron's book *On the Take*.

But the politically-inspired attacks did not end with Mulroney's departure from office, as his unprecedented investigation by the RCMP for allegedly taking bribes over the purchase by Air Canada of Airbus jets required a major libel suit to curtail. Equally unfair, if less noticed outside Quebec, was the persistent persecution of former Conservative senator Michel Cogger, a close friend of Mulroney's, who was finally exonerated only in May, 2001, over charges of influence peddling, but only after having been virtually hounded out of the Senate.

Ironically, another victim of Liberal-inspired image manipulation, at least in Central and Eastern Canada, was Preston Manning, who had happily participated in the demonization of Mulroney in the West when it suited his purpose. Manning, who had always enjoyed a good image in Western Canada — thanks in part to the sterling reputation of his father as premier of Alberta for 25 years — discovered on arriving in Ottawa in 1993, at the head of 51 western MPs and one Ontarian, that his image was already firmly cast in the minds of the press gallery and other central Canadian media as a right-wing fundamentalist western nerd, who looked weird, had a funny voice, and should not be taken seriously as a national politician.

An extremely negative image also preceded Manning into Quebec where from the first, he was portrayed as anti-French and inimical to the vital interests of the province, and where his inability to understand French and his comical attempts to speak it made him a figure of ridicule by the media. He never scored much above one per cent in the polls in Quebec.

The Liberals (and the Bloc Québécois) understand clearly that if you can define the public image of a potentially dangerous opponent negatively, before it can be defined positively by the person in question, the game is essentially over before it starts. At the very least, this makes the task of reversing the initial perception a very difficult one, as first impressions are particularly lasting in politics.

It is instructive to review the ups and downs of Brian Mulroney's approval ratings when he was prime minister. From April 1985 to November 1992, the polling firm Environics asked Canadians three or four times a year, "Do you approve or disapprove of the way Brian Mulroney is handling his job as prime minister?" Here are the results, in both graph and tabular forms.

Brian Mulroney approval ratings graph, 1985-1992
Source: Environics Research Group and Queen's Online Public Opinion Archive

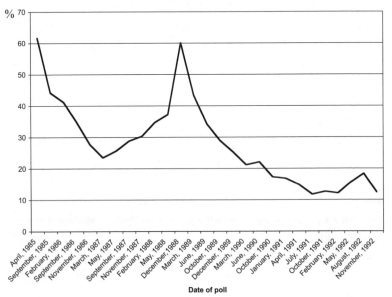

Brian Mulroney approval and disapproval ratings chart, 1985-1992

Date	% who approve	%who disapprove	Don't Know/ No Answer
April, 1985	62	26	12
September, 1985	44	42	14
February, 1986	41	48	11
September, 1986	35	56	9
November, 1986	28	62	10
March, 1987	24	66	11
May, 1987	26	66	9
September, 1987	29	60	11
November, 1987	30	60	10
February, 1988	35	57	8
May, 1988	37	55	8
December,1988	60	24	8
March, 1989	43	45	12
June, 1989	34	57	9
October, 1989	29	62	6
December, 1989	25	67	8
March, 1990	21	73	6
June, 1990	22	72	6
October, 1990	17	79	4
January, 1991	17	78	5
April, 1991	15	79	6
July, 1991	12	83	5
October, 1991	13	82	6
February, 1992	12	83	5
May, 1992	16	80	5
August, 1992	18	76	6
November, 1992	12	83	5

Preston Manning's approval ratings never reached Mulroney's highest levels, because of his poor image east of Manitoba; nor did they reach Mulroney's lowest levels, as Manning never held government office. After peaking at 40% in June, 1994, Manning's approval oscillated between 25% and 34% until finally reaching 38% again when he was building the United Alternative at the end of 1999. But it is interesting to observe the gradual rise in his *disapproval* ratings, beginning at 19% when he was largely unknown outside Alberta in 1991, and rising to 50% in July 1997, as his political opponents and the eastern media did their number on him for the 1997 election.

Preston Manning approval and disapproval ratings graph, 1991-2000

Source: Environics Research Group and Queen's Online Public Opinion Archive

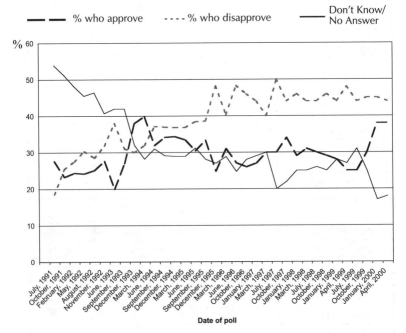

Date of poll

Preston Manning approval and disapproval ratings chart, 1991-2000

Date	% who approve	%who disapprove	Don't Know/ No Answer
July, 1991	28	19	54
October, 1991	23	26	51
February, 1992	24	28	48
May, 1992	24	30	46
August, 1992	25	29	46
November, 1992	28	32	41
June, 1993	20	38	42
September, 1993	27	31	42
December, 1993	38	30	32
March, 1994	40	32	28
June, 1994	32	37	31
September, 1994	34	37	29
December, 1994	34	37	29
March, 1995	33	37	29
June, 1995	30	38	31
September, 1995	33	39	28
December, 1995	25	48	27
March, 1996	31	40	29
June, 1996	27	48	25
October, 1996	26	46	28
January, 1997	27	44	29
March, 1997	30	40	30
July, 1997	30	50	20
October, 1997	34	44	22
January, 1998	29	46	25
March, 1998	31	44	25
July, 1998	30	44	26
October, 1998	29	46	25
January, 1999	28	44	28
April, 1999	25	48	27
July, 1999	25	44	31
October, 1999	30	45	25
January, 2000	38	45	17
April, 2000	38	44	18

7) Since 1993, Chrétien's three Liberal majorities based on Ontario

We have seen that the Liberals' domination of Canadian elections from 1896 to 1980 was based on their electoral strength in Quebec. We have also seen that they lost their Quebec base to Brian Mulroney in 1984, and even more badly in 1988, being reduced to 12 Quebec seats, their historic low. These two losses also cost them the government for nine years. But in 1993, the Liberals regained power, although they took only 19 seats in Quebec. They achieved this by sweeping the larger province of Ontario, a feat never before achieved by any party, but now managed by the Liberals three elections in a row. How did this happen? To understand it fully, we must first re-examine Quebec.

The Liberal Party of Canada is now the world's most successful political party still in office in any democracy. One effect of their long success in Quebec is that the relatively small numbers of Quebec political activists who are interested in federal politics tend to gravitate to the Liberal party. The existence of a strong Liberal party at the provincial level, even if relations between the federal and provincial branches are often strained, also ensures continuity and stability. Since the disappearance of the Union Nationale in the 1970s, no other national party has had a provincial counterpart in Quebec. They have all had to rely on so-called Quebec wings of the national party, and these Quebec wings, whether of the Conservatives, the NDP, Reform, or the Canadian Alliance, have all been woefully weak, except for the Tories during the Mulroney years. The opposite is the case with the Bloc Québécois — the scourge of the Chrétien Liberals — which is completely dependent on the electoral support of the provincial Parti Québécois, and has no independent base of support of its own.

As we have seen, most Quebec francophones are inclined to support a federal party with whose leader they can identify, and that ideally means a fellow Quebec francophone. Party labels, ideologies and policies are less important than personalities. If the array of national party leaders includes only a single francophone, Quebecers will tend to vote for that leader's party (Laurier, St. Laurent, Mulroney). Even if the single francophone leader has no chance of forming a government, he can still do surprisingly well in Quebec, being opposed only by anglophones (Caouette in 1962). If there is more than one francophone leader in the field, it becomes a popularity contest. Trudeau won several popularity contests against a somewhat stale Caouette, whereas Chrétien has lost three times, once to Bouchard and twice to Duceppe. In the one election where there were three francophone leaders (1997, with Duceppe, Chrétien, and Charest), the Parti Québécois machine threw itself behind a stumbling Duceppe, and managed to beat both the still unpopular Chrétien and the popular but bereft Charest who, with no provincial party to help him, still took five seats.

If there are no francophone party leaders at all (last seen in 1958), the Quebec electorate is up for grabs. The Parti Québécois seems to have decided that this situation will never arise again, since by sustaining the Bloc, they will ensure that there is always at least one francophone party leader in every federal election. The leaders of the Parti Québécois understand the value of having an obedient delegation in Ottawa, with the chance that it might one day hold the balance of power. They are likely to continue to support the Bloc, which will continue to do well if the opposing party leaders are all anglophone.

The lesson for the future is that only with a popular leader who speaks fluent French will a national party have a serious chance of winning a majority of Quebec's seats — at least as long as the provincial Parti Québécois remains strong enough to support the federal Bloc Québécois effectively. And as long as the federal Liberals are the only national party with a French-speaking leader, no other national party has a serious chance of winning more than a handful of seats in Quebec. It is this fact that has ensured a secure base for the Liberal party in Quebec, in good times and in bad, and has generally kept the Conservatives in the single digits. Neither the CCF/NDP, nor Reform, nor the Canadian Alliance has ever won a seat in Quebec in a general election.

Ontario, on the other hand, used to provide the most dependable core of Conservative support in Canada. Given the well-nigh perpetual grip of the Liberal party on the federal government, most bright young Liberals have been attracted to Ottawa, and it is not surprising that bright young Conservatives, conversely, tended to concentrate on provincial politics, where they were more likely to be successful. This was certainly the case in Ontario, but also in most other provinces except Quebec. (In British Columbia, where there is no provincial Conservative party to speak of, they moved between Social Credit and the B.C. Liberal Party.)

The successful Ontario Progressive Conservative party has tended to dominate provincial elections since 1943, although well-established Ontario Liberal and New Democratic parties also exist, and each of them has formed a provincial government within the last ten years. Each of Canada's four national parties has a strong organization in most parts of Ontario, and only the Canadian Alliance (and before it Reform) has no provincial counterpart. Given the provincial dominance of the Conservatives, one might think that there would also be a strong Tory contingent from Ontario in Ottawa. Indeed, this was generally the case before the cataclysmic election of 1993. Why, then, is there not a single federal Tory MP from Ontario today?

There are three main reasons. First was the aggressive move into Ontario by Reform in 1993 and 1997, and by the Canadian

Alliance in 2000, which severely damaged the federal Tories without benefitting the newcomers. Second came a falling-out between the federal and provincial Conservative organizations, dating roughly from the 1997 election campaign, which has helped Tory premier Mike Harris rationalize his consistent refusal to play an active role in federal elections. This falling-out was itself the result of several factors, including the view of the Harris Tories that their federal cousins espouse a rather different brand of conservatism from their own, and their understandable reluctance to openly back a losing cause. They also did not wish to engage in a fight with federal Reformers who supported them provincially. The third reason for the three Liberal sweeps of Ontario is the fact that the opposition parties were completely out-manoeuvred by the Liberals who succeeded, brilliantly if unscrupulously, in portraying Kim Campbell, Preston Manning, Jean Charest, Stockwell Day, and Joe Clark as being less in harmony with the interests of Ontario voters than Jean Chrétien.

The popular vote tells the tale. In the face of the Campbell rout and the NDP collapse in 1993, the Conservative vote in Ontario fell to only 17.6%, and the NDP's to 6%. The Reform Party, running candidates in Ontario for the first time, took an impressive 20.1%, but elected only one member. The Liberal party received a whopping 52.9% of Ontario's votes and with them, 98 out of 99 seats. The Tories and the NDP won no seats. We have already looked at the 1993 results in the rest of the country.

8) The 1997 election: the Liberals lose 21 Atlantic seats and 12 in the West, but Ontario gives Chrétien his second majority without winning Quebec

In Ontario, the 1997 election was not much different from that of 1993. The Tories, with high hopes under popular new leader Jean Charest, gained only five points in Ontario, rising to 18.8%, but garnering only one seat. The NDP also rebounded somewhat to 10.7%, but still got no seats. And Reform, reflecting Preston Manning's continuing failure to present an image acceptable to the average Ontario voter, actually declined to 19.1%, losing their lone seat from 1993. The notorious Reform TV ad, with a slash through Quebec politicians, backfired badly in Ontario. Even with a Liberal decline to 49.5%, Chrétien was still able to take 101 of 103 seats, while former Liberal John Nunziata held his seat as an independent.

In preparing for the campaign, the federal Tories had enlisted the help of the team that had recently won the provincial election with Mike Harris, on the plausible theory that they had a good understanding of what motivated Ontario voters. The Harris team was instrumental in preparing the federal Conservative platform, and was ready to jump into the campaign with both feet. At the last minute, however, Jean Charest decided to turn everything over to the tried and true campaign manager of his 1993 leadership campaign, and all further advice and input from Queen's Park was disregarded, as were the contents of the platform. The focus of Charest's campaign shifted from the economy and tax cuts to national unity, as he allowed the Liberals to lure him into talking mainly about the Constitution, which turned off Ontario voters by the thousands.

Tory TV ads, like the rest of their campaign, were unfocussed and ineffective, so that the opportunity for the Tories to make a comeback in their traditional bastion, where they could easily have taken 20 seats with the right campaign, was lost. Within a year, Charest had left to become leader of the Quebec Liberal Party, and former prime minister Joe Clark succeeded him.

East of Ontario, Charest had done much better. The Tories were the main beneficiaries of the collapse of Liberal support in the Atlantic provinces, gaining 12 seats for a total of 13. The

NDP picked up eight seats (six in Nova Scotia and two in New Brunswick), while the Liberals were wiped out in Nova Scotia. They held on to four seats each in Newfoundland and PEI, and three in New Brunswick, for an Atlantic total of 11, just over a third of their 1993 sweep of 32 seats.

In Quebec, as we have seen, Charest took five seats, mostly near his Sherbrooke base in the Eastern Townships, and 22.2% of the popular vote — a higher score than in Ontario. (By the time of the next election, with Charest gone to Quebec City, three of these Tory MPs had joined the Liberal party and were re-elected as Liberals, while the fourth, André Bachand, became the only Tory elected in Quebec in 2000.)

The Liberals continued their slow recovery in Quebec, climbing from 19 to 26 seats, and from 33% to 36.7% of the popular vote. The Bloc Québécois, on the other hand, under new leader Gilles Duceppe (with Lucien Bouchard now the Parti Québécois premier of Quebec), declined to 37.9% of the vote and 44 seats, thereby losing their status as the Official Opposition.

This honour now fell to Reform who, although losing their single Ontario seat and being relegated again to the West, strengthened their position in every western province to win 60 seats. The Liberals lost 12 seats in the West, including six in Manitoba and four in Saskatchewan, to finish with only 15, while the NDP increased their western contingent from eight to 12. Chrétien retained his majority (barely) with 155 seats out of 301, while the NDP came fourth with 21 seats. The Tories gained a seat in Manitoba, bringing their national total to 20 seats — hardly the great comeback the party had been counting on — and still leaving the party of Macdonald, Diefenbaker and Mulroney in fifth and last place for the second election in a row.

The five parties in the House of Commons were now more regionally differentiated than ever. Almost two-thirds of the

Liberal seats were from Ontario, although they still had representation from every province except Nova Scotia. All of Reform's seats were in the four western provinces; all of the Bloc's were in Quebec. While the NDP had a few seats in each of five provinces, they had none in Ontario or Quebec, and had no strong base. Of the 20 Conservative seats, 18 were east of the Ottawa River. Four years after the destruction of the Progressive Conservative party, Canada was no nearer to restoring anything close to a two-party system, and the Liberal party remained without a serious challenger.

The 2000 election campaign was to be an even worse litany of dashed hopes and missed opportunities. All sides knew that Ontario would be the decisive battleground; it seemed inconceivable that Chrétien could pull off a third consecutive sweep of the province.

How his opponents let him do so will be examined below.

The United Alternative Movement, the Canadian Alliance, and the 2000 Election

The Creation and Defeat of the Canadian Alliance, 1997-2000; the Election of November 27, 2000

After two successive failures to break into Central and Eastern Canada, Preston Manning realized after the 1997 election that he and his western-based party, no matter how strong they might be in the West, could not win seats in the rest of the country, particularly in Ontario, as long as the Progressive Conservative party continued to run candidates and divide the anti-Liberal vote there. At about the same time (April 1998), Jean Charest, who had steadfastly refused to cooperate with the man he blamed for the destruction of his party in 1993 and for the "anti-Quebec" television ads of 1997, succumbed to the siren song to accept the leadership of the Quebec Liberal Party. Manning saw an opportunity to bring together supporters of the two parties in a grand "united alternative" to the Liberal party, and possibly even to achieve the organic fusion of the parties themselves. Unfortunately, he had reckoned without Joe Clark.

1) The United Alternative movement, 1998-2000

At the end of May 1998, Manning proposed to the Reform Assembly in London, Ontario that an invitation go out to "all persons like-minded" to attend a giant gathering of representatives of all the various anti-Liberal elements in the country who might consider themselves to be conservative, either fiscally or socially. The Reformers present endorsed the idea to the tune of 91.3%, and in September, a steering committee was established to organize a "United Alternative" convention, including members of the Reform Party, the Progressive Conservative Party of Canada, the provincial Progressive Conservative parties of Nova Scotia, Ontario, Manitoba and Alberta, the Bloc Québécois, the Saskatchewan Party, and the Liberal Party of British Columbia. The non-Reformers on the steering committee (a majority) soon obtained the consent of the Reform members that, in any discussions about a possible merger or formation of a new party, everything must be "on the table" and open for discussion: the party principles and program, the party constitution, the party name, and the party leadership. Despite concerns among his membership that everything Reform had stood for might be lost, Manning could not deny the logic of his new collaborators' position, although he did insist that the leadership be the final issue to be raised, only after agreement had been achieved on all other matters.

However, the United Alternative movement was seriously crippled from the outset when Tory leader Joe Clark, who had succeeded Jean Charest in November 1998, stubbornly refused to participate — or to allow his party to do so in any official capacity. This did not stop large numbers of federal Tories from attending the first United Alternative convention in Ottawa in February 1999 as individuals, including MPs Charlie Power from Newfoundland, lone Ontario MP Jim Jones, and former party president (now senator) Gerry St. Germain. A number of senior Ontario PCs in favour of uniting the two parties also came together as the Blue Committee, under chairman Bob Dechert, strongly supporting the UA initiative.

While Joe Clark even dismissed an invitation to explain his own position to the meeting, Alberta Tory premier Ralph Klein was a strong early supporter of a merger between the two parties, and agreed to be a keynote speaker. Premier Klein used his Friday night speech to the audience of over 1,500 to advocate that any reconstituted party, if it truly wanted to succeed, should recognize Quebec's unique character, while avoiding divisive issues of social conservatism. Speaking as one of Canada's most successful politicians, Klein said, "We cannot, as those who adhere to conservative philosophy, declare ourselves to be the party of minimum interference in the everyday lives of everyday Canadians, and then propose to interfere in the most personal of all decisions."

So it was that the Ottawa convention went ahead without Joe Clark — although John Crosbie attended to denounce the proceedings, colourfully but to no effect — and was a resounding media and organizational success. Major speakers included Alberta treasurer Stockwell Day (fluent without notes), and Quebec nationalists Rodrigue Biron and Jean Allaire, while Preston Manning confined his role to a wrap-up speech at the end of the weekend.

On the Sunday morning, delegates voted to approve or reject four coalition options that had been presented the day before: form a new party; cooperate at the local riding level; rally behind an existing party; or merge under one of the existing parties. The new party option received 55% of first choice votes (665 votes), and was rejected by under 20%. The second most popular option was local riding initiatives, which had been supported in a powerful speech on the Saturday by former Ontario lieutenant-governor Hal Jackman. Accordingly, the 21-member steering committee was authorized to organize and convene a founding convention for a new political party, with which the Reform party and other parties would be asked to join, to be followed by a leadership election.

2) The creation of the Canadian Alliance and Stockwell Day's election as leader, 2000

True to their principles of direct democracy and "grassroots" control, the almost 65,000 members of the Reform party had to approve any next steps. In March 1999, a 20-page booklet entitled *Opportunity Knocks* was sent to every party member, explaining the movement to form a new party, and including a mail-in ballot asking: "Do you want the Reform Party of Canada to continue with the United Alternative process? Yes or No." Replies were due by May 31, and 32,099 ballots were received, for a participation rate of 49.7%. The approval ratio was 60.5%, despite the activities of an anti-UA group calling themselves GUARD — Grassroots United Against Reform's Demise. All regions except Saskatchewan and the North-West Territories returned a majority in favour of continuing the UA process.

Joe Clark had succeeded in keeping his Progressive Conservative party out of any merger, but he was still concerned at the growing support in some of his riding associations for local cooperation with the new party, in order to prevent the election of Liberals through vote splitting between two "small-c" conservative candidates. Accordingly, he had the October general meeting of his party in Toronto amend the party constitution so as to require the nomination of a Progressive Conservative candidate in every one of Canada's 301 federal constituencies, thus effectively preventing any electoral alliance, and ensuring once again the election of a Liberal majority government. Ironically, in the 2000 election, the Tories succeeded in nominating only 291 candidates, ten short of their target of 301, despite their new Clark-inspired constitutional obligation.

Preston Manning, in contrast to Joe Clark, campaigned diligently for acceptance of the new party by Reformers, who would eventually have to hold a second mail-in ballot on whether or not

Reform should formally merge with the new party. On January 8, 2000, Manning sent a letter to all Reform party members saying that he would quit as Reform leader if his vision of a new national party was rejected in this second referendum in March. He was not without opponents. Reform MP Jake Hoeppner had already been suspended from the caucus in July for attacks on Manning's leadership. On January 11, Reform MP Dick Harris said he would run against Manning for the party leadership, and Reform party chairman Gee Tsang announced his resignation over the UA. On January 19, Reform MP Lee Morrison said he would also run for the leadership, and would try to force a leadership election within Reform itself.

The founding convention of the new party took place in Ottawa at the end of January 2000. Stockwell Day delivered another strong speech, this time focussing on the importance of maintaining principles, and extending a hand to Reformers opposed to the merger. He also performed a karate kick on stage that made TV clips and front pages everywhere. Highlights of policy discussions included approval for a 17% single rate of federal income tax, as well as support for official bilingualism and for respecting the rights of minorities (both changes from previous Reform policies).

The other major speech of the convention belonged to convention co-chair Tom Long, architect of Mike Harris's two Ontario victories. Receiving five standing ovations during his Friday afternoon address, Long turned many heads and whipped the crowd into a frenzy with a blistering attack on Tory leader Joe Clark: "For years, Joe Clark has lectured conservatives, tiresomely lectured conservatives about the unfashionableness and unsaleability of their beliefs. He has spent his entire career looking to forge alliances with literally any group but conservatives and he has no meaningful record of accomplishment in promoting the things conservatives care about. The reason for this is quite simple: Joe Clark is not a conservative."

On the night of Saturday, January 28, Preston Manning gave what was billed as the most important speech of his political career. Urging Reformers to "THINK BIG" (eight-foot high letters spelling out this phrase hung behind him), for 70 minutes he reviewed the history of political realignment in Canada, with an emphasis on the accomplishments of Reform since its birth in 1987. He said, "Reform means constant change. Always thinking big rather than thinking small, always accepting risk rather than avoiding it, in order to move ahead."

On Sunday, the convention approved a name for the new party: the Canadian Reform Conservative Alliance, to be commonly known as the Canadian Alliance. Once again, Joe Clark tried to sabotage the success of the movement by having his party launch legal proceedings to prevent the party from using the word "conservative" in its name.

The convention appointed a new national council to manage the Canadian Alliance, composed of the members of the executive council of the Reform party and the members of the UA steering committee, which yielded a good balance between former Reformers and others. Each executive position (president, first and second vice presidents, treasurer and secretary) was filled by two co-equal members of the national council, one from Reform and one not, for a total of 10 executive officers.

When the convention adjourned, the Reform party took over the hall for its own assembly, at which delegates voted 75% against holding a leadership review, confirming their endorsement of Preston Manning's strategy. The next and final step was the submission to the entire Reform membership of the proposal to have the party join the Canadian Alliance, by a second mail-in ballot due March 17. This required the approval of at least two-thirds of the total membership, and a majority in at least seven of the 10 party regions. To the surprise of many, on March 25, 2000, Manning proudly announced that Reformers had given the plan their overwhelming support — 91.9% of party members had voted in favour, easily carrying all 10 regions. The risk of a strong rump party of GUARD dissidents had been averted. Henceforth, only Joe Clark and his band of followers would boycott the move to unite conservatives against the Liberals. Unable to succeed themselves, they determined to act as spoilers to ensure the failure of the Canadian Alliance.

The leader of the new party was to be elected by all party members directly, with $10 memberships being available until seven days before the first ballot on June 24, 2000. It was generally assumed that Preston Manning would have a huge advantage with the support of the vast majority of Reform's 65,000 members. But as the only declared candidate, Manning didn't want a coronation, and made personal efforts to attract strong candidates into the race from other regions. At least partly because of his perceived strength, almost none came forward, and in the end, the only Reform MP to challenge him was Dr. Keith Martin, who announced his candidacy on April 6.

While Ontario activists made frenzied efforts to find a credible Ontario candidate to oppose Manning, Stockwell Day saw his opportunity and exploited it brilliantly. He formally announced his candidacy on March 28. By presenting himself as a more cool, more telegenic and less cerebral version of Preston Manning, but still a bona fide western conservative, he was able to attract many Reformers who had concluded that Manning would never be acceptable to central Canadians. With his rudimentary but serviceable French, and his strong religious connections, he appealed to many Ontario and Quebec conservatives as well. He obtained the endorsement of his premier, Ralph

Klein, and as importantly, the backing of Klein strategist Rod Love and Calgary business leader Gwyn Morgan.

Having been so prominent in January, Tom Long was under great pressure to run in March. He had many reasons to refuse — no French, a young family, and a strong commitment to Mike Harris — but he knew that an Ontario candidate was essential for the future electoral credibility of the party. When other provincial ministers such as Tony Clement, Bob Runciman and Jim Flaherty declined to run, Frank Klees was finally persuaded to step up to the plate, only to back out at the last second when his financial requirements could not be guaranteed ahead of time. Under the circumstances, Tom Long had little choice but to run himself, despite his handicaps and misgivings.

But by that time it was too late. When Long eventually announced his entry on April 27, Day and Manning had already sewn up most western votes, and many Ontario supporters as well. Long's only hope was a massive membership drive, but this went tragically wrong when some recruiters in Quebec signed people up without their knowledge, resulting in improbably high numbers of applications being submitted to the party's Calgary office from the region of Gaspé. This strange news was promptly leaked to the media, and the resulting firestorm finished Long's chances.

On June 24, the results of the first ballot were: Stockwell Day, 53,249 (44%); Preston Manning, 43,527 (36%); Tom Long, 21,894 (18%); Keith Martin, 1,676 (2%), and John Stachow, 211. There had been 120,557 valid votes cast — by far the largest electorate in any leadership race in Canadian history. The Manning camp was stunned, the Day camp exultant, and the Long camp, having seen the writing on the wall, stoic in defeat. Since the runoff vote two weeks later was to include only the top two finishers, Long and Martin were eliminated. Long knew that Day's lead was insurmountable, and a less principled man would immediately have endorsed the undoubted winner. But having recently watched Day closely on many platforms, and having witnessed Day's refusal to disavow base personal attacks by his supporters against Long's friends, Long was among the first to discern the fatal flaws that would eventually bring Day down. Refusing to back Day, Long campaigned tirelessly during the ensuing two weeks for Preston Manning, whom he had come to admire greatly.

Others, less perceptive, jumped on the Day bandwagon, including the Blue Committee and senator Gerry St. Germain, who announced he would leave the Tory caucus to sit as the first Alliance senator. Day easily won the second ballot on July 8, with 75,324 votes (63.6%) against Manning's 43,163 (36.4%). Total valid votes cast were 118,487, only a slight slippage from the turnout on June 24.

After over two years of upheavals and superhuman efforts, and belying the predictions of most observers, a new party had been created and had successfully chosen a new leader, in an impressive series of demonstrations of direct democracy. Most participants were looking forward to a short break before the looming main event — the next federal election. But there is no truce in politics, and in mid-August, a stir was created by Alliance national council member John Mykytyshyn's politically incorrect taped comments that, "People in the eastern provinces believe in handouts and 'Give me a cheque for doing nothing.' They don't want to do what all of our ancestors did, and that was work for a living and go where the jobs are. So probably the Alliance won't go over as well there." With copious Liberal help, this promptly became a self-fulfilling prophecy.

On August 17, former Manitoba cabinet minister and federal PC leadership candidate Brian Pallister defected to the Canadian Alliance: he would become an MP in November. On September 7, after interminable dithering and equivocation,

Jim Jones, the lone Tory MP from Ontario, did the same: he would be defeated in November by a Liberal. On September 11, both Joe Clark (finally, almost two years after becoming PC leader) and Stockwell Day (two months after becoming CA leader) entered the House of Commons through by-elections. Later, three Tory MPs from Quebec announced that they would be running as Liberals in the next election: all would be re-elected in November.

Meanwhile, the Liberal high command watched and schemed.

3) The demonization of Stockwell Day in the eastern media, 2000

Stockwell Day had ridden a long way on the theme of his leadership campaign: "an agenda of respect." Having cut his political teeth in uniformly Tory Alberta, and in the gentler league of provincial politics, he had never experienced the full force of a national (read: eastern) media hatchet job. He seemed unaware how easily his social conservative views, which generally played well back home in Red Deer, could be caricatured by his opponents to portray him as a dangerous extremist. Although he may not have been so naïve as to think that the national media would always treat *him* with respect, he was completely inexperienced in how to defend himself against the inevitable onslaught. Indeed, he barely tried to defend himself at all, allowing the negative image-building by his opponents to proceed virtually unchecked.

Preston Manning had suffered much the same treatment when his party burst onto the national scene with 52 seats in 1993. Our national opinion-makers do not like to be surprised — and they resent even more any successful politician who has not received their prior blessing. Like the Liberal party, they have little understanding of Western Canada, and little interest in what strange cabals might be forming there until they actually risk disturbing Central Canada's comfortable pre-eminence. Although Manning claimed he had eventually learned to deal more adroitly with questions about his social conservative views, he was arguably crippled beyond recovery from the outset in Eastern Canada, by the unfair image of extreme social conservatism pinned on him by the Liberals and the media in those early months.

Here are just six of the most blatant examples of how Day's opponents were able to use compliant media outlets to "define" his public image in central Canada in a most negative and politically damaging way.

(a) Globe and Mail *page one interview with André Turcotte, June 28, 2000; CTV and CBC interviews with Preston Manning, July 4, 2000*

In an interview with Brian Laghi of the *Globe and Mail* published on June 28, 2000 (between the two leadership ballots), Reform party (and Manning) pollster André Turcotte reflected on Day's vulnerability, in a last-ditch attempt to weaken his support and bolster Manning's: "Mr. Turcotte said studies after the 1997 election found that many Canadians refused to vote for Reform because they harboured deep reservations about its social policies, particularly its attitudes toward gays and women. The surveys found, for example, that 60% of Canadians actually supported the notion of gay marriage, while female voters were concerned that the party wanted to turn back the clock in the area of gender roles. 'The big image problem that we had was the perception that the Reform Party was too extreme. It was the major obstacle for the party to governing,' he said. 'Women basically perceived that we wanted to go back to the 1950s.' He also said that, although

Canadians were tolerant of individuals' religious views, they were concerned that Reform had a secret agenda to implement many of its more controversial policies."

While this may sound eerily prescient of the general election campaign to come, Turcotte was simply revealing publicly what both he and the Liberal strategists had long known privately: Reform and Manning had quickly and effectively been branded by their political opponents and the eastern media with a fatally negative public image, particularly in Ontario. While the pollsters and pundits knew that this negative public image of Reform and Alliance policies and positions was a gross exaggeration and distortion of the reality of these policies, they had also learned from experience how easy it is for a clever and ruthless opponent to use compliant media outlets to "define" a politician's public image in this negative way, and how difficult such an image is to shake off. They could see Stockwell Day sleepwalking into the same trap, just as André Turcotte felt that Preston Manning's image was beginning to recover, after years of effort.

The article added that Turcotte "said the three-year effort to broaden the party's base will be wrecked under Mr. Day, and he will likely resign if Mr. Day wins. 'I don't want to be part of fighting another image problem,' Mr. Turcotte said. 'I have better things to do.' (…) Mr. Turcotte said yesterday that a party under Mr. Day risks making the same mistakes that were made in the 1993 and 1997 elections, when it was unable to break out of its western stronghold. 'We're back to square one three years later,' Mr. Turcotte said. 'Actually, we're back to negative square one.' Mr. Turcotte predicted that a party under Mr. Day may also turn off moderate members of the federal Progressive Conservatives. Most of these individuals will either stick with the Tories or opt for the federal Liberals, with whom they will feel more comfortable."

The Manning advisers who had witnessed his own evisceration knew what was in store for Day, but they seemed only too willing to help the process along, rather than give the new leader the benefit of their experience. Perhaps they were too heartsick about Manning's loss to Day to do much to help, and perhaps Day was too consumed by hubris to listen. Strangely, André Turcotte's very predictions, public as they were, themselves fed the process of defining Day's image as an extremist, and helped his prophecy to fulfil itself. A more experienced, more savvy and less self-absorbed politician than Day could have ensured that Central Canada's first (and enduring) impression of him was very different, and proved Turcotte wrong. But as in a Greek tragedy, the protagonist ignored the prophecies of the Cassandra, and the initiated have since watched enthralled as his intrinsic flaws and overweening pride have led inescapably to his preordained destruction. Like Tom Long, André Turcotte had clearly foreseen the most likely denouement long before most others.

On July 4, 2000, just days before the final leadership ballot, both CTV and CBC drew on the André Turcotte interview in questioning Preston Manning about Stockwell Day's "image problem". In questions of the "When did he stop beating his wife?" variety, both Valerie Pringle and Tom Kennedy referred to Day's scary views, without specifying precisely what they might be (see quotes at the end of the next section).

(b) Maclean's "HOW SCARY?" *cover, July 10, 2000*

Day's Achilles' heel was his openly pro-life position on the issue of abortion. This horrified most of the national media, and they quickly leapt to the defence of mainstream (read: their own) values. First of the major news organizations off the mark was *Maclean's* magazine (circulation 506,000, readership 1,700,000), with a textbook example of media complicity in negatively defining a politician's public image. The trick is to use outlandish headlines, "play" (illustration and promotion) and positioning to multiply the impact of a purportedly objective report. Accordingly, *Maclean's* devoted the entire cover of its issue of July 10, 2000 to the great cause. Against a lurid purple background, huge letters asked "HOW SCARY?" The sub-head was "Meet Stockwell Day, the mystery man who would be prime minister." Inside, a short piece by John Geddes was entitled "The Scare Factor: Is Stockwell Day too extreme for mainstream Canadian voters?"

For anyone so obtuse as to have missed the editors' point, the actual article begins with a three-year-old girl, Martha, and her father Greg McNeely, coming out to meet Day. "Asked why he brought his family out to meet the candidate, McNeely expressed his hope that if Day becomes prime minister, he will preside over a national referendum on abortion. (…) Day heads into the stretch run of this race fighting the scare factor. Charges that his anti-abortion, anti-gay-rights opinions will repel mainstream voters broke into the open last week. And even if his surging leadership bid plows past claims that his social conservatism makes him unelectable, Liberals are waiting to pounce on his advocacy of a flat tax and more powerful provinces as equally likely to turn off many voters. (…) If he wins, it will prove that Alliance members decided he wasn't too scary after all. How many other Canadians can be similarly reassured would then be a question for the federal election Prime Minister Chrétien is expected to call this fall or next spring."

A Day sympathizer, or even a mildly analytical reader, might note the guilt by association with an advocate of a referendum on abortion (not Day's position), the repetition of "charges" that Day would "repel the mainstream" and "claims" that he is "unelectable" (both lifted from the *Globe* interview with Manning supporter André Turcotte), and finally the inside knowledge of Liberal strategy. And a westerner might wonder which voters would be likely to be turned off by having "more powerful provinces"? Certainly not voters in the West or in Quebec. But the not-so-subtle message to Ontario is: Ah well, if those western nutbars in the Alliance still insist on making this wacko leader of the opposition, it will just have to be up to us mainstreamers, as the only true guardians of the national interest, to make sure he gets whipped in the election in Ontario at least.

The following week, of course, the editors of "Canada's national magazine", realizing that they might have been just a little too obvious, and to rehabilitate their pretense of even-handedness, ran another lurid cover, this time on Jean Chrétien, asking "HOW CROOKED?", with a sub-head "Is this Québécois too corrupt to be trusted once again with 100 Ontario seats?" The accompanying article pointed out that like Day, Chrétien was also pro-life and opposed to abortion. Funny how nobody saw that issue — because it never happened.

The height of the image manipulator's art is to brand a politician with a negative image in the media, while simultaneously predicting that it will scare voters; then to ensure that it does; and then to blame the victim's failure on his poor image — all the while pretending innocence, or at least invoking the protection of the herd. Revisiting this question after the election, *Maclean's* editor Robert Lewis enlisted other media figures and Preston Manning himself to imply that Day's negative image was all of his own making, and that the media had little or nothing to do with it. In his December 11 issue, reprising the golden oldie headline "Stockwell Day and the scare factor" that had so wowed 'em in July, Lewis wrote:

"On July 4, Valerie Pringle, co-host of CTV's *Canada AM,* asked Preston Manning, then campaigning for the Alliance party leadership, 'How much of an image problem would the Alliance have with Stockwell Day as leader, given his views on homo-sexuals and on capital punishment, abortion, other issues?' Manning's response: 'Well, Reform wrestled with all of that, as you know, from 1993 to 1996. And I learned how to handle those issues. I learned how to express those values on behalf of people to whom they are very important, including myself, but in a way that was respected by other people and didn't scare people that some agenda was going to be rammed down their throat.'

"That night on The National Magazine on CBC, reporter Tom Kennedy asked Manning: 'Is there a risk that Mr. Day has scared off voters because of his views?' Manning's reply: 'Well, there is always that danger.'

"Fear of Day's agenda clearly was a major factor in Jean Chrétien's striking majority victory in the Nov. 27 election. Day was not able to shake the image of a man who was a follower, not a leader, willing to govern by constant referendums on the most divisive issues. Obviously the country is not ready for such an ill-defined approach on social issues such as medicare and abortion."

Things were otherwise fairly quiet in the other "national" media before the election call, except for the occasional pre-dictable diatribe by columnists such as Susan Riley in the *Ottawa Citizen*, Michele Landsberg in the *Toronto Star*, not to mention the venerable (and inevitable) Dalton Camp in the same paper — all blasting Day for his perceived intolerance.

(c) Globe and Mail *"two-tier health care" front page headline, October 31, 2000*

But once the election had been called on October 22, the media slams picked up in earnest. Next up was the *Globe and Mail*, which on October 31 carried a screaming banner headline on page one: "Alliance supports two-tier health care". This was news to the Alliance. The accompanying article by Shawn

McCarthy began, "A Canadian Alliance government would support the development of a two-tier health-care system, with a universal public system supplemented by private clinics, Alliance campaign co-chairman Jason Kenney says." But Jason Kenney had never mentioned "two-tier health care". All he had done was to repeat long-standing party policy that provinces should be allowed to expand the use of private clinics if they so choose. The *Globe* combined this with a similar statement by health critic Val Meredith to concoct its notoriously dishonest headline, knowing exactly how damaging it would be in Ontario at that stage in the campaign. The *Globe* also took this opportunity to give a platform to health minister Allan Rock, who wasted no time in telling the reporter that the Alliance plan would be "fatal to our national system of public health care."

Even *Globe* staffers were embarrassed at the blatant distortion in the October 31 headline, which most ascribed to the ongoing battle with the *National Post*, seen as a supporter of the Alliance.

(d) Toronto Sun *front page headline* "MAYOR: I FEAR STOCK DAY", *November 8, 2000*

Next it was the turn of the *Toronto Sun*. Not to be outdone by less serious Toronto media, on November 8, the *Sun* gave over its front page to its biggest story of the campaign — a real scoop: Toronto Mayor Mel Lastman had told the *Sun* editorial board that Stockwell Day "scares me." The huge page one headline was MAYOR: I FEAR STOCK DAY, with a smaller sub-head saying, "But Lastman says he's never even met the Alliance leader." Inside, on page 16, the headline read: "Is Stockwell scary? asks Mayor Mel; Lastman's unease with the Canadian Alliance leader surfaces at *Sun* editorial board." An accompanying article by none other than editor Lorrie Goldstein himself offered the following quotes to explain the *Sun*'s entirely under-standable excitement and alarm:

Lastman: "I'm afraid of the Alliance. I don't know what this Alliance group is all about, I really don't. I'm afraid of some…"

Goldstein: "What makes you afraid?"

Lastman: "…things I hear. I don't know. This leader, he scares me."

Goldstein: "Why? Why does he scare you?"

Lastman: "Only from what I've heard, only what I've read, and only what I've…I don't know, I've never met him, but…"

(e) *Elinor Caplan claim that Alliance supporters "are Holocaust deniers, prominent bigots and racists", November 14, 2000*

All of the national media reported the most savage and vicious slander of the campaign, by Liberal attack-dog Elinor Caplan, who tried to tar the entire Canadian Alliance with racism on November 14. According to the *Toronto Star* of November 15, "Liberal immigration minister Elinor Caplan launched a blunt attack at the Canadian Alliance yesterday, labelling some of the party's supporters bigots and racists. Speaking to a boisterous party rally in Thornhill last night, Caplan said the Alliance is a reflection of the people who support the party. 'Their supporters are Holocaust deniers, prominent bigots and racists,' Caplan told the crowd. The minister, who is in a tough political fight to keep her Thornhill seat for the Liberals, said the Liberal party does not want those people in its ranks. 'These are not the values of the Liberal party and we don't want them,' she said to the cheering crowd. Markham Liberal candidate John McCallum, who's on leave as chief economist with the Royal Bank of Canada, said immigrants are not embraced by the Alliance the way they are by the Liberals. 'At best, the Canadian Alliance tolerates the presence of new Canadians,' McCallum told the crowd of more than 500 people. Both Caplan and McCallum were part of a warm-up act for a speech by Finance Minister Paul Martin, who did not touch on the immigration question or the Alliance's position or possible links to extremists.

"Caplan risks losing some support in her riding after the Jewish community responded angrily to Canada's decision to support a United Nations resolution condemning the Israelis for their part in recent violence in the Middle East. Caplan also finds herself facing a strong threat from the fact that the Jewish community is interested in Alliance's promise of tax credits for parents who send their children to denominational school. After the rally, Caplan said her comments stem from the Alliance's known associations with people who are Holocaust deniers and racists. 'You can tell who a person is by the people who support him,' she said, citing, as an example, plans floated by Alliance incumbent Eric Lowther of Alberta to call for a citizen referendum on immigration. 'That kind of opinion — that anti-immigrant, racist, bigoted opinion — is not something that the Liberal party would tolerate and it says a lot about Stockwell Day and his supporters.' Caplan said Day's own history as a supporter of a Christian curriculum in a religious school in Alberta is suspect. 'As a teacher in the accelerated Christian education curriculum, the province of Alberta found that the curriculum discriminated against aboriginals, against blacks and against Jews. We should be concerned about someone who would defend that curriculum.'"

Yet, as the *Star* and Caplan both knew would happen, Caplan won her seat by a larger margin than she had in 1997, with 64.6% of the vote, against 15.8% for Alliance candidate Robert Goldin, her closest rival. Caplan got 27,152 votes, and Goldin was next with 6,643 votes. Some tough fight.

(f) *CBC "documentary" by Paul Hunter on Stockwell Day's religious beliefs, aired on* **The National,** *November 14, 2000*

Probably the most damaging piece of character assassination of the whole campaign was an extraordinary CBC "documentary" on Stockwell Day's religious beliefs — a first for Canadian political journalism, especially in the middle of a tight election. Although the reporter never spoke to Day or his family, he repeated a number of unsubstantiated hearsay comments attributing various statements and actions to Day. The program covered Day's history in the village of Bentley, Alberta, and parts of his political past:

"It's where Day first mixed religion and politics, and he's been asked ever since whether the two should mix." (…) "Whether you call it family values, Christian morals or theo-conservatism, Day as politician espoused it here." (…) "It was reported here that Day once called homosexuality a mental disorder. Now as leader of a national party, he's denied that.

"In fact, over the years in politics Day has made his opinion known on a variety of moral touchstones. He's spoken out against abortion — once, saying that women who get pregnant through rape or incest should not get government-funded abortions unless their pregnancy is life-threatening. In 1994, he supported a book ban in Alberta schools calling the language in *Of Mice and Men* 'blasphemous'. And on how to best deal with criminals such as mass murderer Clifford Olson, he told a conference in Calgary three years ago, 'People like myself say, fix the problem. Put Olson in the general prison population. The moral prisoners will deal with him in a way we don't have the nerve to.'"

Then came the knockout punch. Over a sketch of unidentified heavenly bodies, reporter Paul Hunter intoned: "But of all the views expressed by Day over the years, there is one from which literally everything else flows: his belief in how it all began. It came out during a speech he gave in 1997 at Red Deer College during 'Christian Awareness Week.' It was billed as a talk about evolution. Professor Pliny Hayes took his class in for a listen and to this day he and some of his students can hardly believe what they heard."

Prof. Pliny Hayes: "He prefaced his comments with a smile and a question, 'Are any of my friends from the press present?' When no one responded, he then went on to say a number of things — one, that the Earth is 6,000 years old, that Adam and Eve were real people, that humans co-existed with dinosaurs, that there is as much evidence for evolution, or for creationism rather, as there is for evolution, and that he's upset that creationism can't be taught in public schools."

Paul Hunter: "He said those words?"

Prof. Pliny Hayes: "He said those words. There are a number of social issues, controversial social issues — abortion, death penalty — about which honest, well-meaning people will have different opinions, and their opinions are often formed by their religious beliefs, and I think that's absolutely appropriate. But here we're not talking about things that are a matter of personal opinion. The age of the Earth is a subject of scientific inquiry. There's a mass of scientific data on the age of the Earth, and it all says that the Earth is between four and a half and five billion years old — and that it is not, that it could not be 6,000 years old. It is absolutely clear that humans did not exist with dinosaurs. And as for creationism and evolution, there is a mountain of evidence which says that evolution happened, there is simply no discussion of that in biology."

Unfortunately, according to journalist and author Clare Hoy, many of the hearsay comments reported by Paul Hunter were inaccurate. In his book *Stockwell Day: His Life and Politics,* Hoy says with regard to *Of Mice and Men,* "The thing is, it wasn't Day who wanted the book banned, it was the Red Deer South MLA,

Victor Doerksen. Day said at the time that children 'don't need to be exposed to the name of Jesus Christ being taken in a blasphemous sense,' but he did not advocate banning the book. He did say Doerksen had the right to represent that view on behalf of his constituents." (pages 70-71)

With regard to government-funded abortions, Hoy explains that in 1995, Day joined 16 other cabinet ministers and MLAs in agreeing with the Committee to End Tax-Funded Abortions that was calling for an end to tax-funded abortions except in cases when the mother's life was at risk. Hoy continues, "Critics immediately attacked Day for wanting to cut funding even to victims of rape and incest, and to this day journalists — and Day's political opponents — continue to repeat this charge against him. In her June 14, 1999 *Calgary Herald* column, for example, Susan Ruttan wrote, 'presumably he (Day) thinks raped women should do their civic duty and bear the unwanted child.' Again Day denied saying it, and nobody in the media had actually quoted him — or produced a quote later on — using the words *rape* and *incest*. Reporters had inferred it because Day had said many couples were eager to adopt, 'be it a product of any situation.' In fact it was Day's Red Deer South colleague, Victor Doerksen, who had mentioned rape and incest. But even there, Doerksen had explained to a reporter from his local newspaper that abortion funding by Alberta Health wouldn't be necessary in cases of victims of rape and incest, because the Alberta Crimes Compensation Board would cover it. He said that it was 'a moot point' from a financial viewpoint because 'in those cases, compensation is already available,' That detail was ignored in the ensuing outcry by pro-choice advocates and their media supporters." (page 72).

Reflecting on the CBC's journalistic ethics, *Edmonton Journal* columnist Lorne Gunter wrote on December 13, 2000:

"The Canadian Broadcasting Corporation aggressively promoted the 'hidden Alliance agenda' mantra as devised by the Liberal war room. In perhaps the most shameless (and shameful) example of a media outlet trying to manipulate the outcome of a Canadian election, the CBC broadcast an alleged investigative report on Stockwell Day's fundamentalist, creationist beliefs at exactly the point in the campaign at which the one-sided anti-Day piece would do the most harm to the Alliance and the most good for the government. Moreover, the CBC aired it without even once asking Day for his reaction to the allegations contained therein, or without at least seeking an academic or scientific expert sympathetic to Day's ideas." Such is the fate of a politician who dares to suggest a partial privatization of the CBC.

On November 16, 2000, the Liberals returned to the attack during a panel discussion on CTV's *Canada AM*. Seizing the opportunity to ridicule Stockwell Day on the basis of the Pliny Hayes comments given such prominence by the CBC two days earlier, Liberal panelist Warren Kinsella showed the camera a fuzzy children's toy known as Barney, the purple dinosaur. According to the *Ottawa Citizen* of November 17, "Mr. Day has said...that dinosaurs walked the Earth with humans," Mr. Kinsella said as he produced the Barney doll. "I just want to say to Mr. Day that the Flintstones were (*sic*) not a documentary and the only dinosaur that walked with human beings recently was this one right here." Once your opponents can get away with that kind of mockery, your credibility as a political leader is finished.

4) The premature 2000 election - the Liberals seize their opportunity

How to win a modern election campaign: define your opponent's image, manage the campaign dialogue in your favour, and introduce wedge issues that divide the enemy forces

A modern election campaign is a struggle to create media images. Political parties and candidates try to create a favourable image for themselves, while trying equally hard (or harder) to blacken the image of their opponents. Meanwhile, the media try to avoid being mere tools of the party image-makers, and increasingly engage in image manipulation of their own. Since television is still the most effective medium for instilling images of politicians in the minds of voters (most of whom are not paying much attention), a campaign consists essentially of a series of highly artificial events involving party leaders, plus paid television advertising. The whole purpose of the various leaders' so-called "tours" is to gain favourable coverage on TV, as well as in the press and on radio. The Internet is becoming increasingly significant in political image-making, but it is still far from matching the power of the nightly television news. Twenty-four-hour news channels also protect the dominance of TV, allowing instantaneous messaging at any time.

The media, of course, know exactly what is going on. Although they resent being "used" by the parties as mere vehicles for propaganda, they cannot entirely boycott the daily staged leaders' events. So they retaliate by frequently refusing to relay what the parties want them to, and instead they have become full actors in the play themselves, creating and conveying the images they themselves feel are appropriate under all the circumstances. In the circus atmosphere of a leader's tour, any pretense of media objectivity is soon lost, as reporters and editors push their own agendas, and party flacks attempt to induce them to carry their candidate's intended message while ignoring or ridiculing the other side's.

There are two great commandments in the game of political image-making. The first and greatest of these is never to let your opponent, or hostile elements of the media, "define" your public image, for obvious reasons. The corollary is to do your own utmost to define your opponent's image — negatively. The public image of any candidate consists of an amalgam of positive and negative impressions, or "favourables" and "unfavourables", and the most effective way to destroy the image of your opponent is to "drive up the unfavourables", in the jargon of the pros. This is because, as we saw in Chapter 8, people are far more inclined to believe negative information about a politician than positive. Hence, the popularity of negative political advertising and various other forms of character assassination. It may not be pretty, but it works — unless the other side can succeed in making it appear unfair or excessive, as in the case of the Tory TV ads in 1993 mocking Jean Chrétien's mouth. Going negative is still an art, not a science; and as in any art, most practitioners are journeymen, while a few are superb virtuosos.

The second is like unto it, namely this: always manage or control the dialogue or the topic of debate, and never let your opponent or the media force you onto dangerous terrain. This means keeping the discussion on issues which are favourable to you, and harmful to your opponent, while keeping the focus away from your own weak points. A candidate who loses control of the debate is in the dreaded position of being forced "off message" and "onto the defensive"; as a result, each side is constantly trying to sandbag the other with accusations it hopes are sufficiently credible and inflammatory to make an impression on undecided voters, forcing the other side to respond. The media, on the other hand, are less fastidious about the credibility of any charges, and are generally happy to broadcast them as long as they can cite a "usually reliable source who wishes to remain anonymous." After all, if the accusation blows up, it is the politicians, not the media, who will get hurt. In fact, this is the part the media love most, as they can exaggerate, over-dramatize and embroider such charges to their hearts' content, doing their gleeful best to escalate the battle, while pretending all along that they are simply the messengers.

Finally, the most effective way to shatter your opponent's support is to drop into the dialogue of the campaign what is descriptively called a "wedge issue". This is an issue on which there is disagreement, or at least potential disagreement, among groups who are otherwise in the same camp. Obviously each side wants to keep its own divisive issues off the table, while attempting to divide the other side by exploiting its wedge issues. In the 2000 election, the neutron bomb of wedge issues was abortion. As long as the abortion issue did not figure in the campaign, Stockwell Day had a chance of holding together a coalition of voters in the key battleground of Ontario who were all sufficiently fed up with the Liberals for one reason or another to vote for the Alliance, even if without much enthusiasm. But if abortion ever became an overt issue, and his own pro-life position the question on which people's votes would turn, then the many defenders of a woman's freedom of choice who might otherwise support Day could be split away from him.

If, through the clever use of these techniques, you can succeed in branding your opponent with an image that is on balance negative, so that most undecided voters have an unfavourable opinion of him or her by election day, and if at the same time you can keep the focus of attention away from your own failings, then you can probably make your opponent the main issue in the campaign, turning it into a referendum on his or her suitability for office that is already lost.

The Liberal advantages in the fall of 2000

Much of the behaviour required for a successful media campaign is counter-intuitive, and can only be learned from experience. For example, it is human nature for a gregarious political leader to like schmoozing with the press corps accompanying his tour, and to be constantly available for questions and interviews. Big mistake. All that does is water down the message, and create opportunities for distracting stories or even worse. What is required is absolute discipline and tightly controlled access to the leader, so that the only image or message that the media get is the single one the campaign wants. It is also human nature for the various advisers and handlers accompanying the leader, or back at campaign headquarters, to want to talk to the media too, either to give their "spin" on events or to feel important and involved. Another error, as this makes for a number of apparent campaign spokespersons instead of just one, with inevitable contradictions and confusion.

In the end, the leader's tour, and the campaign's fixed nerve centre or "war room", must be run along strict military lines, with a clear and inviolable hierarchy and chain of command, and complete centralized control over communications. It takes time and experience to build a team that can function smoothly in these circumstances, and to gain the familiarity and trust with one another that are necessary to work together efficiently under pressure.

In the fall of 2000, the Liberals knew that their greatest advantages lay first, in Stockwell Day's personal inexperience in the role of party leader in a national election campaign, as opposed to Jean Chrétien's many successful national campaigns, including two as party leader; and second, in the strength of Chrétien's battle-hardened campaign team, which had worked together for years, in contrast to the Alliance leader's lack of any team at all — most of Preston Manning's experienced senior advisers being either not interested or not wanted by Day, and key members of Day's leadership team being unavailable.

The situation facing the Liberals when Parliament resumed in September 2000 was almost ideal. Unlikely to get any better later in the mandate, it soon proved too good for the prime minister to resist. Because of Joe Clark's miscalculation about the success of the United Alternative movement, the opposition was still divided among four mainly regional parties, all devoting resources to fighting one another as well as the government. Because of Preston Manning's miscalculation concerning his own chances of retaining the leadership of the Canadian Alliance, Jean Chrétien faced a new and inexperienced leader of the opposition, who could be counted on to make the mistakes of a neophyte. Because of Tom Long's miscalculation in entering the Alliance leadership race too late, the opposition leader was once again from Western Canada, instead of being a pillar of the Ontario PC party, whose team might have inflicted some serious damage on the herd of Liberal MPs from Ontario.

Once again, the mistakes of his adversaries had played into Jean Chrétien's hand. After toying with Stockwell Day in the House of Commons for a few weeks, and trapping him into calling for an immediate election, on October 22 the prime minister exercised his right to request the dissolution of Parliament even though he had a year and a half left in his mandate, and the election was called for November 27, 2000. Stockwell Day had been leader of the Alliance for only two and a half months.

The 2000 election: a disaster for the Alliance and the Tories; Ontario gives Jean Chrétien his third majority

The ensuing campaign was an object lesson from the Liberal team on how to run a successful election, and from the Alliance team on how not to. Suffice it to say that the Liberals succeeded brilliantly (often with Day's apparently unwitting complicity) in negatively defining the media image of Stockwell Day, while Chrétien's

opponents barely laid a glove on him, despite his glaring vulnera-
bilities. Day was thrown off message and onto the defensive four
or five days each week, often in response to a complete absence of
discipline in the Alliance camp. Joe Clark and Alexa McDonough
happily piled on Day as well, apparently unaware that their own
base was also being eaten away by the Liberals.

When, for a brief moment, the Alliance appeared to be
gaining ground in Ontario, approaching the magic 30% mark in
the polls that would begin to yield seats, the Liberals ruthlessly
raised the abortion issue by having the prime minister tack it on
to the end of a speech in Montreal, and were able to accuse Day
of having a secret agenda to remove women's rights to freedom
of choice through a binding referendum initiated by his religious supporters. Liberal pollster Michael Marzolini later
reported to a party meeting that his nightly tracking showed that
from that moment, Alliance support, particularly in Ontario,
began dropping like a stone.

Again, it was Alliance amateurism, lack of discipline and
central control of its campaign that gave the Liberals this
opening. The official Alliance platform had contained a brief
mention of the intention to introduce measures to "allow
Canadians to bring forward citizen-initiated referendums." But
although never official party policy, a background briefing book
prepared for candidates by the Alliance research office went
further in discussing how such referenda might work.

On November 7, a page one headline in the *Globe and Mail*
trumpeted "Day's plan found in secret paper". The article by
reporter John Ibbitson began, "Under the prime ministership of
Stockwell Day, Parliament would hold a free vote on marijuana
use, natives on reserves would lose their sales-tax exemption,
the CBC would be put up for sale, and 25 per cent of the voters
in a riding could unseat a member of Parliament. These and

many other policies are contained in the official but confidential policy background document sent to Canadian Alliance riding candidates in the coming federal election. A copy of the document has been obtained by the *Globe and Mail*." An accompanying page one article headed, "Abortion issue ignited by Alliance document…" added, "As abortion vaulted to the centre of the federal election campaign yesterday, Canadian Alliance leader Stockwell Day appeared at odds with his party's campaign material over how much popular support would be needed to force a referendum on the divisive issue."

The briefing book said that a petition signed by three per cent of the electorate from the previous federal election might be sufficient to trigger a referendum. After an Alliance candidate confirmed that this figure had indeed been discussed, it became the basis for every conceivable conjecture and scenario, including CBC-TV comedian Rick Mercer's call on Monday, November 13, on *This Hour Has 22 Minutes*, for Canadians to sign a petition on the Internet demanding a referendum on whether Stockwell Day should be required to change his name to Doris Day. By Thursday night, nearly half a million people had voted on the website, and by Friday, the figure had reached 616,000, although not all were of voting age. Three per cent of the electorate in 2000 was 637,304 voters.

But perhaps the most damaging effect of the media treatment of the Alliance briefing book was the credibility it lent to charges that the Alliance, and particularly Stockwell Day, had all kinds of dangerous "hidden agendas" which they did not want to reveal to the public, but which they would move to implement once they were elected. In his December 13, 2000 retrospective in the *Edmonton Journal*, columnist Lorne Gunter wrote, "When the *Globe and Mail* was given an Alliance candidates' briefing binder it acted as if it had uncovered an enormous conspiracy to defraud the voting public. The information in the binder was specifically designed to be used by candidates (all parties have them) to answer questions about Alliance policy from reporters and voters. In other words, the policies in it were not 'hidden' in any way. Its contents were no more designed to be kept from the public than the dialogue in a play is meant to be kept from the audience. But the Liberals charged that the binder revealed a hidden agenda and much of the media followed that line dutifully."

Gunter, a rock-ribbed conservative, observed, "The Liberals, to their great success, throughout the election painted the Canadian Alliance as a gang of dangerous wing-nuts with more hidden agendas than a prairie has gophers. None of the allegations were true. An Alliance government would not have recriminalized abortion, or disbanded medicare (too bad), or privatized the Canada Pension Plan (pity), or made school prayer mandatory, or institutionalized anti-Semitism, or converted Canada into a Christian theocracy, or herded immigrants into concentration camps. All of these suggestions, though, direct and implicit, were levelled by Liberals against the Alliance, and dutifully and mindlessly repeated by reporters across the country as though they were incontrovertibly true."

In the end, most Ontario voters — especially the women — although largely disgusted by the campaign itself, concluded that Jean Chrétien was the lesser of two evils, and that they had better vote for him to keep that scary Stockwell Day as far from power as possible. Having seen his credibility destroyed, Day was now helpless to deflect his opponents' charges. Writing in the *Globe and Mail* on November 9, Margaret Wente best summed up the mood of women in particular, who were being viscerally repelled in droves by the image of Day that the Liberals had so ruthlessly crafted. There was "not a chance" that Canadian women would support Stockwell Day's "Reform-

Alliance", the columnist wrote. "Nearly all the women I know are convinced that, *no matter what he says*, Mr. Day's Agenda of Respect includes a hidden agenda to roll back the right to choose. And they are not going to let him get away with it." (Emphasis added.) She and many others had swallowed the Liberal line, and it worked to perfection.

Another example of how Alliance naiveté was effectively exploited by Liberal cunning, duplicity, and spin is the sad story of Betty Granger, a highly respected school trustee who was the Alliance candidate in Winnipeg South Centre. On November 16, 2000, Betty Granger attended a political science seminar at the University of Winnipeg, at the invitation of political science professor Allen Mills. Prof. Mills had contested the Crescentwood constituency for the Liberal party in the last provincial election, finishing last of the major candidates. During her talk, which *supported* Canada's need for immigration, Betty Granger was unwise enough to twice use the phrase "Asian invasion", adding, "that may not be the best wording." Sensing blood, and knowing that there had been no media present at the seminar, Prof. Mills notified a friend in the Liberal party, Heather Mack, who quickly obtained a tape of the seminar from the university's information desk.

As Betty's brother Dennis Owens wrote in the *Winnipeg Free Press* on February 14, 2001, "This story was fed by the Liberal party to Toronto media. The instant headlines were the beginning of a series of events that smashed Betty's campaign and destroyed her political career. Mills assisted the media circus with sanctimonious comments about the intolerance of the Alliance party, even though he'd witnessed the whole seminar."

As the Alliance campaign staggered, battered and bleeding, toward the finish line, it was hit with one final body blow. On November 23, four days before the vote, the *Edmonton Journal* carried a front-page story by reporter Tim Naumetz headed, "Alliance would phase out old age security: Policy manual says party also intends to scale back CPP." The article, which was immediately picked up by all the national media, began, "The Canadian Alliance plans to end the old age security benefit and scale back the Canada Pension Plan while allowing more room for investment in private retirement plans, a senior Alliance MP says. While maintaining the universal OAS payment of $428 a month to seniors already receiving it, the Alliance plans to reduce it incrementally for younger Canadians, to the point where those now aged 20 to 25 would not get it by the time they retire, Alberta MP Ken Epp, a deputy finance critic for the party, said Wednesday. 'The OAS is a government program and I think as we come up with alternative methods of providing for people's income when they reach retirement age, we would have to phase that out,' Epp said in an interview. (...) Canadian Alliance campaign brochures, including a detailed manual distributed confidentially to the party's candidates, do not specify the party's proposals for the $23.4 billion Ottawa spends annually on the OAS, guaranteed income supplements and spousal allowances. The glossy Alliance brochure published for voter scrutiny promises a 'long-term look' at retirement policy and the appointment of a non-partisan commission on retirement security and 'generational fairness.' (...) The party's internal campaign manual suggests candidates tell questioners the party will 'honour our obligations to retired Canadians and maintain support for low-income seniors' and note Finance Minister Paul Martin attempted to reduce retirement benefits through the aborted introduction of a consolidated seniors benefit plan in 1998. Both publications state an Alliance government would increase contribution room for RRSPs to 30 per cent of income from the current limit of 18 per cent. *But Epp's comments indicate the Alliance has privately already determined how it will eliminate the OAS."* (Emphasis added.)

As a demonstration of how to shoot yourself in the foot, Mr. Epp, incumbent Alliance MP for Elk Island, Alberta, could hardly have done better. But according to the *Journal*, he plowed on: "'Just off the top of my head, without reading the section, our plan is to basically grandfather everybody who is in it now, but (phase it out) for people who are young and have adequate time to plan for their future,' Epp said in response to questions about the policy. 'I don't have the party policy right in front of me, but as I recall that's what it is.' Human Resources Minister Jane Stewart, responsible for the retirement security programs, said she was astounded by Epp's statement and questioned why the Alliance has not been discussing its plans for the seniors programs publicly in the election campaign. 'Fundamentally, the OAS is the basic pension that is there for everybody who hasn't got enough; for many women it's all they have,' she said. 'This is shocking. When were they thinking of bringing this out?' Stewart added the government discovered in earlier studies most Canadians want to maintain the fundamental public retirement benefit schemes rather than put more emphasis on large RRSPs. In a later interview, Epp agreed the candidate's manual was not as definitive as his earlier description of the Alliance plan."

At this point, Alliance campaign officials could only sigh in amazement and despair.

On November 27, the Liberal party once again swept 100 seats in Ontario, winning 172 seats overall (but only 17 west of Ontario). The Alliance was a distant second with 66 seats (all but two of them west of Ontario), the Bloc Québécois third with 38 seats, the NDP fourth with 13 seats, and the Progressive Conservatives fifth for the third election in a row with 12 seats, nine of which were in three Atlantic provinces.

Phoney Democracy Ruins CA
Parties ruled by media, not backroom boys or grassroots

Column by Brian Flemming in the Halifax *Daily News*, Wednesday, July 18, 2001 (See also *Method of selecting the leader* in Chapter 7)

When, not if, the Canadian Alliance morphs into yet another party of the right, its founders must step back and ask: can a modern political party have too much democracy?

Too much democracy? How could any party, or any country for that matter, ever have too much of that supreme political good, democracy? Indeed, how much democracy is too much for parties should be one of the great political questions of our time. But it is not — yet.

Long ago, party leaders and policies were picked by insiders, far from cruel TV klieg lights and surging scrums of reporters. The last bastion of that system has fallen in Britain, where leaderless and floundering Conservatives will finally allow electors outside its parliamentary caucus to help choose a new leader.

Canadian parties changed in the 1960s by allowing a broad spectrum of party members to select leaders and policies in open conventions. The rationale was a democratic one: open processes would end the monopoly of backroom boys (not girls) and give "grassroots" activists major roles in choosing leaders and policies.

That made sense in those halcyon days because those grass-roots delegates to conventions were usually people who'd paid their dues by working in elections, mostly for free. They were the canvassers, fund-raisers, envelope-lickers, drivers and head-quarter managers. And they were committed.

WINNER TAKE ALL

But the backroom crew quickly learned the new game. Delegate-selection meetings became battlegrounds where slates of potential delegates, ones committed to particular candidates, were put forward. At local levels, it became a winner-takes-all process. Despite that, delegates still physically attended conventions where they could communicate personally with one another about the qualities of potential leaders or policies on offer. And forge bonds of loyalty.

But democracy again reared its questionable head. Parties purged insider influence by adopting a "pure" one-member, one-vote system. Has it made parties better or more democratic? Sadly, the answer appears to be no. At its worst, the new democratic dispensation has made parties hostage to unstable blobs of shifting, uncommitted members.

In retrospect, the two major losers in these *faux*-democratic processes have been the elected members of caucus and the cores of loyal party supporters. Both groups have lost both prestige and power. In the phoney "new and improved" democratic parties, $10 membership cards, not one's position or track record, became the currency of power.

Instead of relying on seasoned judgments of insiders, the newly-minted, and terribly temporary, card-carriers looked to the media for their opinions, little realizing the media were prone to the dreaded "starling complex". Like starlings who move in flocks from wire to wire, the media move en masse when reporting on subjects *du jour*. Take, for example, the two most commented-upon "stocks" of last year: Stock Day and Nortel stock. Last July, few media mavens could find fault in either: today, both stocks have been consigned to media hell.

Could it be (that) the scribblings of all those "analysts" were about as useful as an ashtray on a motorcycle? Could it be that for party members to rely on the media alone for their political opinions is really anti-democratic because that reliance makes people stay in their societal silos where they are disconnected?

LOSS OF LOYALTY

There's been much hand-wringing in recent years about the sharp decline in political party loyalty and commitment. Who wants to join a party or caucus where opportunities for influence are close to nil and where, when crucial decisions are made, they're made by $10 interlopers with no commitment to anyone but a single (failed?) candidate or policy?

Any new unite-the-right party — plus all existing parties — must look carefully at the wreckage that's been caused to party structure by an excess of phoney democracy. All parties must find new, and perhaps even superficially anti-democratic, ways to deal with unrealistic grassroots expectations so the cruel constitutional circus the CA has had to endure never occurs again.

How to Cooperate and Beat the Liberals

Column by Tom Flanagan in the *National Post*, Friday, June 5, 2001

Canadian Alliance leader Stockwell Day yesterday announced he will ask his party's national executive to hold a party referendum within 90 days on co-operation with the Progressive Conservatives. Meanwhile, dissatisfied New Democrats dream of creating a new vehicle on the left. Indeed, the two efforts are not inimical to each other, because chipping away at the Liberals from both the right and the left may be the only way for Canadians to get any alternation in government.

It's exhilarating to contemplate, but agonizingly hard to achieve, because politics never involves writing on a blank slate. Political parties have to learn to co-operate with each other, putting vested interests, careers, and big egos at risk. It's tough, but not impossible.

Stockwell Day, Joe Clark, Svend Robinson, and all the others talking about the co-operation and reorganization of political parties don't have to reinvent the wheel. Political history offers at least five models that parties can follow if they want to get together. None is perfect, but all are worth considering.

The most minimal possibility is unilateral action, in which one party refrains from contesting certain seats. The British Liberals did this early in the 20th century when they were far bigger than Labour and didn't need any reciprocal concessions. They reasoned correctly that, in a score of industrial ridings, Labour would have a better chance of beating the Conservatives, thus making it easier for the Liberals to form a government. If all else fails, the Canadian Alliance and/or the Progressive Conservatives might unilaterally decide not to challenge the other party's incumbents, or not to run in certain parts of the country.

The virtue of this approach is that a party can go ahead and do it without having to reach an agreement. However, it can be difficult to impose withdrawal upon the party's rank-and-file, and some riding associations might insist on running quasi-independent candidates. Yet, if the number is not too great, unilateral withdrawal can still have a practical effect.

A stronger level of co-operation is the electoral alliance, in which two or more parties devise a common platform and agree to share out candidacies according to a negotiated formula. The Liberals and Conservatives did this successfully in British Columbia in the 1940s to keep the Co-operative Commonwealth Federation (CCF) out of power. The Liberals and Social Democrats did it with less success in the British election of 1987.

An electoral alliance allows parties to keep their identities yet co-operate in a coalition capable of winning an election and governing. One major challenge, in addition to negotiating a joint platform and keeping the grassroots in line, is to sort out who will be prime minister in case of victory. Lack of clarity about who was really top dog helped to sink the Liberal-Social Democrat coalition in 1987.

A still tighter form of collaboration is the federation, in which parties unite under a common leader and create a new legal identity, but keep their identities and organizations as federated elements. The CCF followed this model in 1932, as did the left-wing Alliance party in New Zealand in 1991.

The federation model allows parties to retain separate identities, membership lists, and fundraising structures while uniting under a single leader. It might well seem more attractive to voters than an electoral coalition. However, like a coalition, it would have to allocate candidacies. This wasn't a problem for the original CCF, because it was a federation of parties operating separately in various provinces; but it would be a challenge for the Alliance and Tories, or the NDP and the Greens, who compete directly with each other.

Perhaps the most common approach is to create a new party in the hopes that existing parties can join a new entity more readily than they can co-operate or merge with each other. This is what happened when the Canadian Alliance was created last year, and when the CCF turned itself into the NDP in 1961. No other party joined with the CCF, but organized labour became a powerful partner with a formal constitutional position in the new party.

The new party model is attractive and sometimes successful, but it carries the risk of splitting existing parties without fully absorbing them. This happened to the Canadian Alliance when it attracted the so-called Blue Tories to its banner but left the Progressive Conservatives — battered but still intact — standing to fight the next election. The same would happen in reverse if the Tories reorganized themselves to absorb dissident Alliance elements but could not attract the entire Alliance.

The outright merger of separate parties occurs infrequently

because of the difficulty of melding existing organizations, but it is possible. A recent Canadian example is the two-stage formation of the Parti Québécois in 1968. First René Lévesque's Mouvement Souveraineté-Association merged with Gilles Grégoire's Ralliement National, after which Pierre Bourgault's Rassemblement pour l'Indépendance Nationale joined in.

Outright merger may be the ideal solution, but history shows few successful cases except where the founding partners were small and had little to lose. It is much harder for large organizations already endowed with members, money, and MPs to add the fourth M — merger. There are, however, cases, such as the Canadian CCF and the New Zealand Alliance, where parties founded as federations (preceded to some degree by electoral coalitions) gradually turned themselves into fully merged parties.

So there it is — five models to choose from, each of which can be varied in detail. None may be ideal, but each can work better than the current free-for-all. The first set of politicians to exhibit creative statesmanship in applying these models may succeed faster than anyone imagines in replacing a Liberal government that most Canadians would like to get rid of if they could see a realistic alternative.

Tom Flanagan is professor of political science at the University of Calgary.

Bibliography

Barnes, Paul J. *Engineering Realignment: An Analysis of the United Alternative Initiative*. Honours thesis. Department of Political Science, Faculty of Arts, Acadia University, April 2001.

Beck, James Murray. *Pendulum of Power: Canada's Federal Elections*. Scarborough: Prentice Hall Canada, 1968.

Cameron, Stevie. *On the Take: Crime, Corruption, and Greed in the Mulroney Years*. Toronto: Macfarlane, Walter & Ross, 1994.

Canadian Alliance. *A Time for Change: An Agenda of Respect for All Canadians*. Election Platform 2000.

Canadian Alliance, *Canada Strong and Free: A Defence Strategy for the New Millennium* [Online], Available: http://www.canadianalliance.ca/_pdf/paper.pdf. Accessed May 18, 2001.

Conference Board of Canada, *Performance and Potential 2000-2001: Seeking "Made in Canada" Solutions* [Online], Available: http://www.conferenceboard.ca/pdfs/pp_00kf.pdf. Accessed July 3, 2001.

Courchene, Thomas J. *A State of Minds: Toward a Human Capital Future for Canadians*. Montreal: Institute for Research on Public Policy, 2001.

Dobbin, Murray. *Preston Manning and the Reform Party*. Toronto: James Lorimer and Company, 1991.

Elections Canada. *Reports of the Chief Electoral Officer of Canada, 36th General Election, June 2, 1997* and *37th General Election, November 27, 2000* [Online], Available: http://www.elections.ca/home.asp?textonly'=false. Accessed May 20, 2001.

Elections Canada. *Reports of the Chief Electoral Officer of Canada* (1972, 1974, 1979, 1980, 1984, 1988, 1993). Ottawa: Office of the Chief Electoral Officer of Canada.

Elections Ontario, *Election Results and Statistics* [Online], Available: http://www.electionsontario.on.ca. Accessed June 14, 2001.

Feigert, Frank B. *Canada Votes, 1935-1988*. Durham: Duke University Press, 1989.

Flanagan, Tom. *Waiting for the Wave*. Toronto: Stoddart, 1995.

Gwartney, James; Lawson, Robert; Park, Walter; and Skipton, Charles. *Economic Freedom of the World 2001 Annual Report* [Online], Available: http://www.fraserinstitute.ca/publications/books/efw_2001/. Accessed May 27, 2001.

Horowitz, David. *The Art of Political War and Other Radical Pursuits*. Dallas: Spence Publishing, 2000.

Hoy, Clare. *Stockwell Day: His Life and Politics*. Toronto: Stoddart Publishing Co. Ltd., 2000.

Kaplan, William. *Presumed Guilty: Brian Mulroney, the Airbus Affair, and the Government of Canada*. Toronto: McClelland & Stewart Inc., 1998.

Manning, Ernest C. *Political Realignment: A Challenge to Thoughtful Canadians*. Toronto: McClelland & Stewart Ltd., 1967.

Martin, Roger L. and Porter, Michael E. *Canadian Competitiveness: A Decade after the Crossroads* [Online], Rotman School of   Management, University of Toronto and C.D. Howe Institute, Available: http://www.rotman.utoronto.ca/research/competitive1.htm. Accessed June 13, 2000.

McCallum, John. *Will Canada matter in 2020? Basis for remarks in Lecture Series 2020: Building the Future, University of Waterloo, February 16, 2000* [Online], Available: http://www.royalbank.com/economics/market/pdf/can2020.pdf. Accessed May 25, 2001.

McMahon, Fred. *Retreat from Growth: Atlantic Canada and the Negative-Sum Economy*. Halifax: Atlantic Institute for Market Studies, 2000.

Nevitte, Neil; Blais, André; Gidengil, Elisabeth; and Nadeau, Richard. *Unsteady State: The 1997 Canadian Federal Election*. Don Mills: Oxford University Press Canada, 1999.

Progressive Conservative Party of Canada. *Change You Can Trust: The Progressive Conservative Plan for Canada's Future*. Election 2000 platform.

Reports of the Chief Electoral Officer of Ontario, 1985-2000. Elections Ontario [Online], Available: http://www.electionsontario.on.ca.

Richler, Mordecai. *Oh Canada! Oh Quebec!: Requiem for a Divided Country.* Toronto: Penguin Books, 1992.

Savoie, Donald J. *Governing from the Centre: The Concentration of Power in Canadian Politics.* Toronto: University of Toronto Press, 1999.

Sharpe, Andrew. *A Comparison of Canadian and U.S. Labour Market Performance, 1989-2000.* Ottawa: Centre for the Study of Living Standards [Online], Available: http://www.csls.ca/pdf/sharpe.pdf. Accessed June 3, 2001.

Sharpe, Sydney and Braid, Don. *Storming Babylon: Preston Manning and the Rise of the Reform Party.* Toronto: Key Porter Books, 1992.

*   *   *   *   *

Note: The opinion data utilized in this book were originally collected by Environics Research Group. The data were made available by Queen's University, Kingston, Ontario. Neither the original source nor collectors of the data nor Queen's University bear any responsibility for the analyses or interpretations presented here. 1997 Canadian Election Study data were made available by the Social Science Data Centre (SSDS) in the Documents Unit at Stauffer Library, Queen's University, Kingston, Ontario.

Permissions

About the Authors

PETER G. WHITE

Peter White has been active in Canadian political and business life for over forty years. While at law school in Quebec City, he founded the Laval Congress on Canadian Affairs in 1961. He was later a speechwriter for a cabinet minister in the Pearson government (Maurice Sauvé) and a premier of Quebec (Daniel Johnson *père*). In 1976 and 1983 he worked on Brian Mulroney's leadership campaigns for the Progressive Conservative party, subsequently serving as director of appointments and later as principal secretary to former prime minister Mulroney. In 1966, he gave Conrad Black his first job in the newspaper business, in Knowlton, Quebec. In 1969, he, Conrad Black and David Radler bought the Sherbrooke *Record*, the first of many newspapers which became the Hollinger publishing group in Canada, the United States and England. Most of Hollinger's Canadian papers were recently sold to CanWest Global of Winnipeg. From 1972 to 1990 Mr. White lived in London, Ontario where he owned and operated the London News, and served a term on London city council. Since 1990 he has lived in Knowlton and Banff, Alberta, where he owns the Timberline Hotel and is co-owner of Banff Mount Norquay ski resort. He has been chief fundraiser for both the PC party and the Canadian Alliance, where he is a member of the National Council. Mr. White has served as chair of a number of public policy organizations, and is on the board of several Canadian companies. He is a member of the French Legion of Honour.

ADAM DAIFALLAH

Born and raised in Peterborough, Ontario, Adam Daifallah is completing his final year of a politics and history degree at Queen's University in Kingston, Ontario. Active in both the Ontario PC Party and the Canadian Alliance, Adam has served as policy director of the PC Youth Federation of Canada, president of the Federal PC Association of Peterborough, president of the Queen's University Canadian Alliance Association and as vice president and now president of the Ontario PC Campus Association, the province-wide campus affiliate of the Ontario PC Party. He served as the final student trustee of the Peterborough County Board of Education (1997) and as the first student trustee of the Kawartha Pine Ridge District School Board (1998). A former competitive golfer and curler, Adam has won provincial-level championships in both sports. From 1998 to 2000, Adam wrote a weekly opinion column in the *Peterborough Examiner*, "Adam's Edge". He has since been published in the *National Post, Globe and Mail, Saturday Night* magazine, *Calgary Herald, Ottawa Citizen, Hamilton Spectator* and numerous other publications, both online and in print. He has also appeared as a guest on a number of public affairs programs on both radio and television. This year, Adam was selected as one of the 10 finalists in the Magna for Canada *As Prime Minister Awards* contest, winning $10,000 and a four-month, paid internship at Magna International Inc.